A SMART KID'S GUIDE TO SOCIAL MEDIA, SURFING THE WEB, AND STAYING SAFE ONLINE

A Smart Kid's Guide to Social Media, Surfing the Web, and Staying Safe Online

For permissions or further information, please contact:

The Kindness Company
kindnesscompanymail@gmail.com

Printed in the United States

ISBN: 9798846858220

A Smart Kid's Guide to Social Media, Surfing the Web, and Staying Safe Online

Alden C.B.

Dear parents and educators,

Thank you for trusting me to educate your child about social media and the online world. After years of working with children, and many months of extensively researching social media and the problems it causes specifically in kids and young adults, I truly believe that we must face this social media crisis head-on for the sake of our children's futures. I became inspired to write this book after watching the kindergarteners I was teaching pretend to be "social media models" at recess. At a normal, run-of-the-mill elementary school in Minnesota, these five and six-year-olds were talking about likes and followers and what they would wear in their pretend posts. It shocked and saddened me to think children so young would be thinking about these things, but also made me aware of the fact that we *must* start playing an active role in educating kids on using social media and the internet safely.

Though we may think we are shielding our children from every possible online interaction, it is impossible to do so in this day and age. The average child now has a phone by age twelve or thirteen, but this age is getting younger and younger every year, and our kids are getting smarter and smarter about how to have potentially dangerous online interactions without alerting their parents. It is imperative to start having regular conversations in the home about how the internet impacts our kids and families, as many of these impacts are extremely negative.

I highly encourage you to read this book before giving it to your children. The short stories about the consequences of tech are very real scenarios derived from my own personal experiences or from the experiences of those I know. Some stories may be graphic or intense for younger readers. Though 9-14 is the suggested age for this book, you must decide what age is best for your own child to have them read this content. And though I have thoroughly researched this book, I encourage you to continue researching these ever-evolving issues in your own time.

If you have any questions after reading the book, I refer you to www.stopbullying.gov, a wonderful resource that gives helpful information about specific social media apps and cyberbullying, as well as the laws, policies, and regulations that protect children online. Thank you again for taking the time to educate your child about the virtual world in which we live.

Sincerely,
Alden C.B.

CONTENTS

Before You Read...

Likes! Views! Followers! You've probably heard these words before. And I'll bet you know that they have to do with a word called social media located on...the internet. In this book, you're going to learn SO! MUCH! about the internet, social media, and how to stay safe in the virtual world around us.

It's hard being a kid right now, especially since the COVID-19 pandemic when so many kids (maybe even you) went to school online. You will be using the internet for the rest of your life, and it's important that you learn and understand how to use it in a positive way so that you can keep growing up to be the amazing, fantastic person that you already are!

Lastly, my dear friend, some of the things discussed in this book can get very serious. If you are worried or confused while you are reading, please talk to your trusted adult and have them read the book with you. Though some things online are scary, it is important to talk about them so you can stay safe and be smart in the online world.

WHAT EXACTLY *IS* THE INTERNET?

Say hello to the internet! It's a crazy world where you can find answers to pretty much any question you can think of! It's also a place to explore new creative things and ideas, hear about news from around the world, buy cool stuff, create videos and art, and connect with family and friends. Most adults use the internet for their jobs, and some adults work only online from the comfort of their homes. Maybe this will be you one day!

The original computer was invented in America in the 1960s by the United States Department of Defense. This military agency invented it so their researchers could share information with each other. The first computers that people created to use the internet were GIGANTIC! They filled entire rooms! Thankfully computers and internet-capable devices (like phones, tablets, and e-readers) are now much smaller, some even tiny enough to fit on your finger!

Right now, around 6.3 BILLION people have their very own mini-computers, a.k.a. the "smartphone." That's a lot of phones! And a whoooole lot of screens. Each of these screens is connected to the great big internet.

How many screens do you have in your home?

How many screens do you have in your classroom at school?

The internet is like a big, wide ocean. It stretches as far as you can imagine, and it is very, very deep. There are light, positive, happy things towards the surface of the internet. But as you swim further and further within the internet, things can start to get a little dark. Because the internet is so vast, or big, there are lots of good things but also many bad things that can happen when you're online. This book will help you better understand how to keep yourself safe when you encounter things that do not feel right.

Like an ocean is filled with an almost infinite, or unlimited, amount of water, the internet is filled with an almost infinite amount of information. But unlike the ocean, where you can actually see and touch the water inside, where does the information on the internet live? Is it invisible?

Once information is on the internet, it goes to a real-life physical spot on Earth: data servers. **Data servers** are big machines stored in huge ware-houses called data centers. This is where the information created on the Internet lives, and where it is stored and protected.

To access the internet at your house or your school, you must first connect to the internet.

Internet connection works like this:

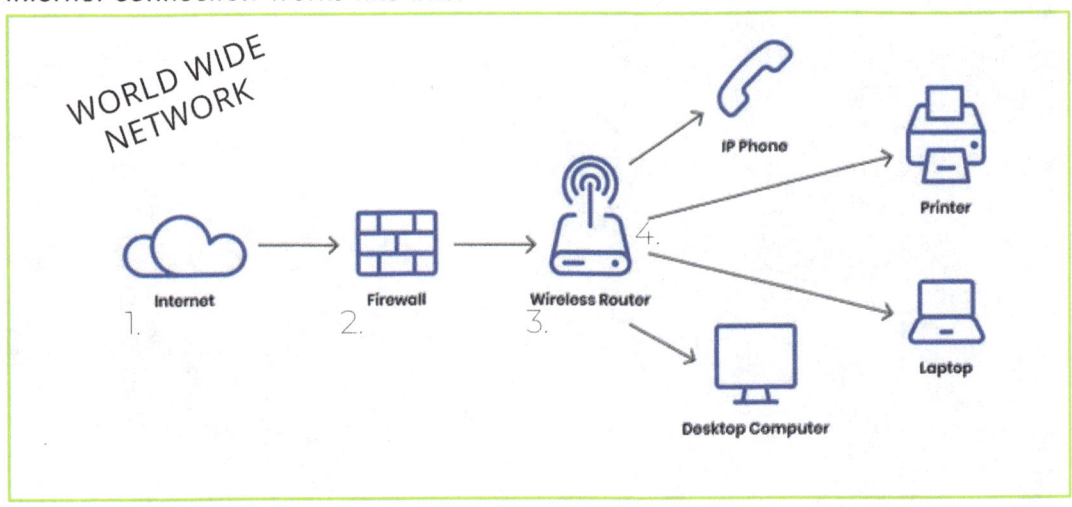

1. The Internet cloud is connected to a worldwide network. The cloud transmits a signal.

2. The signal passes through a firewall. Firewalls are really important because they block unauthorized access while allowing you to communicate with others. In other words, only the good signals are allowed to reach your device because the firewall keeps out the bad signals, kind of like a digital bodyguard.

3. The signal goes to a wireless router, which broadcasts the signal within a certain physical area (like a school or a house).

4. You connect to the wifi signal with your device. Sometimes this requires you to enter a password.

WARNING: It's possible for internet hackers, or people who commit crimes on the internet, to go through firewalls or connect to a public wifi signal. You must always be careful when connecting to public Wifi; it's possible for hackers to use the same signal and hack into your device to access your personal information.

WEBSITES

On the internet, there are different pages called websites where you can go and spend your time. Every website has a name, and this name is called a "domain name". To locate the website, you use its "web address" or the "URL" (Uniform Resource Locator). Some of the most popular websites are Google.com, Amazon.com, and Netflix.com. Many websites are free, but you must pay to use certain websites by buying something called a subscription. A subscription is a service you use that is paid every month. Never buy anything or subscribe to anything online without talking to your parents first.

DOMAIN NAME

send to:
sparklydogs.com

sparklydogs.com

WEBSITE

URL

http: //www.sparklydogs.com

Your **domain name** is your online address, the **URL** leads people to your front door, and the **website** is like an actual house where a business permanently lives.

Many websites will ask you to create an account when you try to use it. If you choose to, you will create a username and password, and enter other personal information like your name and age. It is important for you to know that kids are not allowed to create accounts on most websites without their parent's permission. Always talk with your trusted adult when you would like to create a new account somewhere online, or if you would like to try to find a new website.

Wow! Look how much phones have changed in the past 140 years!

EMAIL

Emails are like digital letters. Just like you must know someone's address to send them a letter or a package, people must know your email address to be able to send things to you. Many adults use email every day to send work-related messages, personal messages, or even to receive notifications about online sales from their favorite stores.

To @crazydinosaurlover4567@bmail.com

Subject Dinsosaur Convention??

Dear Rufus,

It was great to talk to you last week at the science fair. Your project on pollination was really great! I am writing to see if you would like to go to the dinosaur convention with me this weekend. My mom can take us to the convention center, and we can eat lunch afterward at the T-Bone Cafe. Tell your mom to call my mom if you want to come with us!!

Thanks!
Riley

Send

REAL WORLD CHALLENGE!

Before email was invented, people had to send physical letters through the mail using the post office. Make someone's day, and write a good old-fashioned letter or postcard! Pick a friend or a family member and write them a note or draw a picture to send to them. Ask your adult to help you find a stamp and mail your letter!

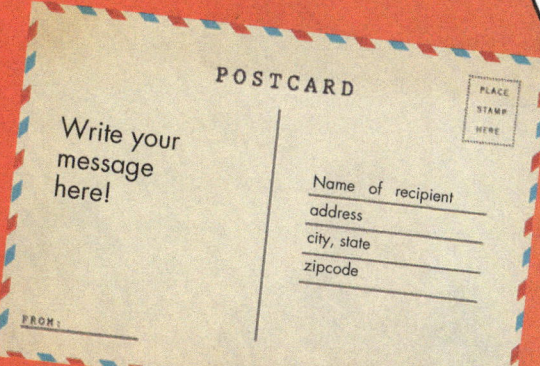

EMOJI CODE BREAK

👽 + 🛳️ = _____

🐮 + 🔔 = _____

🔊 + 🌙 = _____

🐱 + z^zZ = _____

🌴 + 🙈 + 📚 = _____

answers on page 16

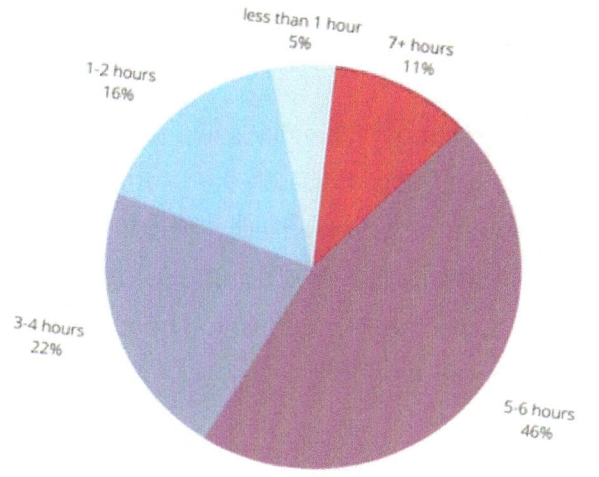

less than 1 hour
5%

7+ hours
11%

1-2 hours
16%

3-4 hours
22%

5-6 hours
46%

7+ HOURS
Lots and lots of screen time!

5-6 HOURS
This is the average for American adults. Wow! Does this number surprise you?

3-4 HOURS
22% of Adults use their phone for 3-4 hours a day. What do you think they use them for?

1-2 HOURS
About 16% of people use their phone for 1-2 hours a day. Does this seem like too much or too little?

LESS THAN 1 HOUR
Only 5% of Americans use their phone less than 1 hour a day.

Average American
Phone Time

WBU?

- HOW MANY HOURS A DAY DO YOU SPEND ON A SCREEN?

- WHAT ARE SOME ADVANTAGES OF SPENDING SO MUCH TIME IN FRONT OF A SCREEN?

- WHAT ARE SOME DISADVANTAGES OF HAVING A LOT OF SCREEN TIME?

- WHAT ARE SOME ACTIVITIES YOU CAN DO BESIDES SCREEN TIME?

USING THE INTERNET FOR HOMEWORK OR RESEARCH

The internet is a great place to learn new things! Many kids like to use the internet for homework, or for researching school projects. Because the internet has so much information, it can be hard to find websites that aren't filled with ads and gross stuff. Remember, there is a lot of real information out there but also a lot of information that is not real. Below are some great websites you can use when researching for school that have real, good information. Ask your parents or trusted adult for help!

- kiddle.co
- kidzsearch.com
- ZAC browser- this website is specifically for kids with autism, who might feel overwhelmed by all of the noise and colors from a regular browser

ONLINE SHOPPING

Getting things in the mail is usually really fun and exciting. You've probably seen someone in your house get something in the mail that they ordered online. Maybe you've even received an online package! Many products and services are now ordered online instead of buying the product or service in a store. Kids are not allowed to buy things online without their parent's permission.

Always make sure you're buying things from a legitimate (real) website. Sometimes, people buy something online and it doesn't show up at their house! This is called a scam. We'll talk more about scams later, and how to figure out if a website is a scam or not.

Answers: 1.UFO 2.Cowbell
3.Soundwave 4.Catnap 5. Jungle Book

LET'S DIG DEEPER: CRYPTOCURRENCY

What is it: a virtual form of money that isn't produced by the government or banks. The prices of the coins go up and down depending on demand, or how badly people want to buy them.

When was it created: 2009

Different Types: Bitcoin, Ethereum, Polkadot. Also called "crypto"

What does it look like: You can't hold crypto in your hand. It doesn't exist in the physical world. In order to own cryptocurrency, you must open an online crypto account.

Crypto farms: crypto farms don't have cows or pigs. They're big warehouses full of computers that "mine", or try to find cryptocurrency.

Environmental costs: It takes a LOT of energy to mine cryptocurrency. In fact, a single crypto transaction is estimated to burn 2,292.5 kilowatt hours of electricity, enough to power a typical US household for over 78 days!! Because so much energy is used, cryptocurrency isn't very friendly to the environment. The industry is working towards making crypto more sustainable, and better for our earth.

DON'T BE TRASHY...

Did you know that 20 to 50 million metric tons of e-waste are disposed of worldwide every year? Always make sure to bring your used electronics to an electronic recycling plant. Call2Recycle.org can help you find a local drop-off bin when it's time to recycle your next phone or tablet! There are also programs where you can donate your used electronic device to someone in need. Doing a little research before tossing a device in the trash can really make a difference for our planet!

PHOTOSHOP

Something you will encounter online is called "photoshop" or "photoshopping". This is when someone takes a picture and changes it in some way by using digital software. Here are some examples:

Can you tell what's been photoshopped into the pictures above? In the first picture, there is a bird with a cat's face- this isn't real! There is also no desert next to a green pasture. The third picture shows you how photoshop can be used to change someone's appearance. Someone digitally added makeup to the woman when she wasn't wearing any in real life.

You can see in these examples how realistic photoshopping images have become. This is why you must always be suspicious of what pictures you see online. It's very hard to tell if they're real or fake!

DEEPFAKE

A new digital technology has emerged in recent years, called *deepfake*, or *deepfaking*. This very advanced technology allows creators to make fake videos and media that look very real. Deepfake technology can take a real-life video and merge it with a fake video. The new deepfake video looks real, but isn't.

For example, there are lots of videos of Zendaya online. Deepfakers could take a real-life video from the internet, and create an entirely new video where Zendaya says "I like cheesy fries and bingo!" Now, who knows if Zendaya really **does** like cheesy fries and bingo; the point is that people no longer have to really say things for there to be video evidence. The video will look real, but it's not!

Another example is when movies like Star Wars need to have a character in the film, but the real-life actor has died. Movie creators can deepfake the face of the original actor onto a real-life actor, and it looks like the dead actor is still alive!

How do you spot a deepfake video? Though the technology is getting better and better every day, there are some tricks you can use to spot a deepfake.

• The audio doesn't sync perfectly- the person moves their lips to different words than the audio.
• Unusual shadowing- the shadow doesn't match the picture.
• Pixelation- the video looks grainy or "off" somehow.
• The information doesn't match what you know to be true.

Think logically about what you see online, and always check other credible news sources to figure out if a video is real or fake.

Ask a parent to scan this QR code with their phone. It'll take you to a news video discussing and showing examples of deepfake.

ARTIFICIAL INTELLIGENCE

Artificial Intelligence (A.I.) is like having a robot or a computer that can think and learn on its own. It's a type of technology that helps machines to do things that we humans can do, like seeing, talking, and even making decisions. For example, you might have seen a voice assistant like Siri or Alexa on a phone or a speaker. They use A.I. to understand what we're saying and give us answers to our questions. A.I. can also help us solve problems, like figuring out the best way to get somewhere or helping doctors to diagnose diseases. It's pretty amazing how much A.I. can do!

While A.I. has many amazing possibilities, it's also important to be aware of some potential dangers. Just like how we need to be careful with fire or electricity, we also need to be careful with A.I. One danger is that A.I. might learn things that are harmful or unfair because it learns from the data it's given. Another danger is that A.I. might become too powerful and we might be unable to control it. That's why scientists and engineers are working hard to make sure that A.I. is safe and helpful for everyone.

- Siri - Siri is a voice assistant created by Apple that uses A.I. to answer questions and carry out tasks. You can ask Siri to set reminders, play music, or give you directions.

- Alexa - a voice assistant created by Amazon that can help you with everything from playing games to controlling your smart home devices. It uses A.I. to understand your requests and respond naturally.

- Google Assistant - a voice assistant created by Google that uses A.I. to help you with tasks and answer questions. You can use it to check the weather, set reminders, or even control your smart home devices.

- Midjourney - an art-generating A.I. platform from a website called Discord. It allows users to create amazing artwork from text descriptions.

- DALL-E- an A.I. program created by OpenAI that can generate images from text descriptions. Like Midjourney, DALL-E uses machine learning to understand the relationships between objects and create new, unique images from text users submit.

- ChatGPT - an A.I. program created by OpenAI that can hold conversations with people and write in many different kinds of styles. Schools have had problems with students using ChatGPT for their homework! Do you use ChatGPT already? Though it might be tempting, it's important for us as learners to not rely on technology to do the learning and writing for us. Otherwise, we won't know how to do anything!

LET'S TALK!

Have a discussion with a friend or family member about A.I.

1. What is A.I. and how is it different from regular computers?
2. Can you think of any toys or games that use A.I. to make them more fun or interesting?
3. How do you think A.I. knows how to do things like recognize faces or play music?
4. Why is it important to be careful with A.I. and make sure it is safe?
5. Can you think of any jobs that might be done by A.I. instead of people?
6. How do you think A.I. could be used to help us solve problems like pollution or hunger?
7. Is it possible for A.I. to become too smart and start making its own decisions?
8. Why is it important to treat everyone fairly when we use A.I.?
9. Do you think A.I. will become a normal part of our lives in the future?
10. What would you like to learn more about A.I.?

Social Media is a type of website or application (app) that lets users create and share content and have online connections. Let's look at some important terms to know in order to better understand social media.

Content	Pictures, videos, wirings, music, and other media that can be shared online
Post	The act of putting content on social media for followers to see
Followers	Real-life people that see what is posted on your profile
Friends	Another word for followers. Could be your friend in real life, but could also be someone you only kind of know, or don't know at all!
Profile	The screen on the app or website that often shows your username, name, a profile picture, and your bio
Bio	Short for "biography". Usually 1-2 sentences explaining who you are. Can be funny and tell a joke instead or simply have emojis
Post	The act of putting content "live" for your followers to see
Like	Double-tapping the screen on the post. Will usually "heart" the post to show you've like it

Views	How many people have seen a post
Viral	A post that has lots and lots of views (1 million or more)
Feed	The main screen of the social media website or app
Scroll	Moving up and down through your feed
Selfie	A picture taken of yourself with the camera flipped around
Handle	the name of your profile, how others find you. Often begins with an @ (ex. @fluffytrees)
Block	Banning a person from seeing your profile or content. If someone is being mean to you online, you can always block them
Comment	Writing a message in response to a post, located underneath a post
Caption	The text underneath a post that describes or goes along with the post
DM	Stands for "direct message". You can DM people on most social media apps to send them private messages
Private vs. Public	You can set your profile to be private or public. Private means only your followers can see your posts. Public means anyone on the app or the website can see your posts
Tagging	Someone can "tag" you in a post. This means that they put your handle in the post. Others can see if you are tagged. (Ex. Your friend posts a picture of you and them, and they put a tag on your face to show others who you are)
Virtual Reality	Also called "VR". A fake environment which is experienced through the senses (such as sights and sounds) provided by a computer and in which one's actions can control what happens in the environment

SOCIAL MEDIA PLATFORMS AND DIGITAL CONNECTIONS

For most of human history, people had a really hard time staying in touch with the people they met over the course of their lives. That friend you had in third grade? You'd most likely never see or talk to them again after elementary school. The nice neighbor you had growing up who let you pick their strawberries? Again, you'd probably never see or talk to them ever again if you moved away.

This all changed in 2009, with the rise of social media. Suddenly, you'd be able to find little third-grade Sheila, or even the strawberry neighbor, Mr. Jones. You could see what had happened in their lives if they had kids or grandkids, and all of the other things they were up to! How exciting! During the first wave of social media and social connection platforms, it was a joyous celebration of finding the people in your life that had long been lost by time and the waves of life. Social media even connected long-lost family members, reuniting and solving age-old family mysteries. For the first time EVER in ALL of human history, people were able to connect easily with others across the entire globe!!

The Negative Side Effects

You may have heard the saying "There are two sides to every story," and this is definitely true when it comes to the story of social media. On the one hand, social media gives people the opportunity to make meaningful virtual connections with people they don't know in real life who have the same interests or hobbies, and also to follow their real-world friends' and relatives' lives. Social media also has very creative users called "influencers" who create content on everything from home decor to science facts to delicious recipes.

It can be very inspiring to see all of the ideas people have online, and may inspire you to create or learn something new in your own life!

However, with the good also comes the bad. One of the most stressful things about being on social media is the fact that you're usually only seeing people at their best. Their best hair day, their best outfit, their most awesome accomplishment. Everyone struggles in life at some point or another, but social media users usually don't like to post about the boring or bad things in their lives. Social media can make you think that you're the ONLY person who has problems, or bed-head, divorced parents, or acne. This can make us feel lonely and isolated. It also makes us have a distorted, or twisted, view of the world around us. When everyone's life online looks perfect, it can make us think that something is wrong with us when life isn't going our way.

Always remember that social media is FAKE! People pick and choose what they post to make their life seem the most interesting or the most perfect, when in reality their life may not be as perfect as it seems.

Social media also takes a lot of TIME. We'll talk more about this later, but the number-one goal of every social media platform is to take as much of your time as possible. If they take your time, they can often get you to spend money on an advertisement you see, or by getting you to pay for advanced features on the app. Being intentional about how much time you spend on social media can really help. Don't spend your time scrolling through pictures of your friend's cousin's weird-looking dog if you don't really want to do that. Use social media to connect with the people you'd like to connect with, and then take a break.

You and your family will have to decide if social media is right for you. There are millions of families that choose NOT to have social media accounts: there's a lot of creepy people online! There's even a growing movement among young people to delete social media apps from their devices and disconnect from digital connections in order to make real-world connections instead.

 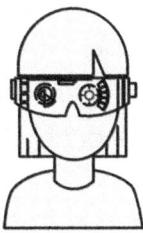 

UIRTUAL REALITY
AND THE METAUERSE

The metaverse is here! An interactive, digital world where the internet comes to life, the **metaverse** is accessed with a virtual reality headset, also known as "VR". When you have a VR headset on, your eyes are completely surrounded by a screen, and everything you see, hear, and experience feels very life-like.

THE METAUERSE

The metaverse is kind of like a video game, but much more life-like and in real-time. For example, in The Metaverse and virtual reality, it will be possible to play soccer with your friend even though your friend is not in the same room as you, if both you and your friend are wearing VR headsets. You will be able to talk to each other and communicate like you were actually hanging out in person. You'll be able to see yourself kicking the ball and the sounds of the stadium around you. You could even play your soccer game in outer space or on a distant alien planet!

Virtual reality is going to become bigger and bigger in your lifetime, and you and your parents are going to have to decide if it's right for your family. We don't yet know all of the bad things that are going to come from this new technology, so we need to start using it carefully and thoughtfully.

do i know you?

Sometimes it might feel like you know someone online REALLY well. Maybe you've watched their videos a thousand times, or have followed them online for years and years. Maybe you know the names of all of their family members, and their favorite food, and have heard stories from their childhood.

Though you may think you know an influencer or video creator super well, you don't. Unless you've met them in person, and have had a conversation with them in person, you don't know who the influencer is behind the screen. Like a superhero when they put on their cape, most internet creators have a "persona," or a public identity, that they project to their followers. This identity is often very happy and positive, exciting and funny!

In reality, internet creators are just like you and me and struggle with all of life's ups and downs. Influencers are not your friends. Friendship requires a two-way relationship, where both people give and take (it also requires in-person time together!). Don't ever think that someone you follow online is your friend, even though they might say they "love" their followers. Content creators don't love you. They love the fact that you're engaging in their content and making them money. They love the fact that you're giving them a job by looking at the content they create.

#VIRAL CHALLENGES

Every now and then, a new viral trend happens online, where you'll record yourself completing a task and then post it. A lot of these challenges are really fun! But some of these challenges can be really, really dangerous. Some kids have even died from doing viral challenges that they didn't understand.

Always make sure you know the risks before completing a challenge, and talk to a trusted adult to make sure you won't get hurt.

Better Get Watching...

Did you know that every 1 minute, about 100 hours of video is uploaded to YouTube, the internet's biggest video streaming website? Because of this, it's physically impossible to watch every video! But if we stopped the uploads, it would take you about 94,643 YEARS to watch the current 829,000,000 hours of video available. Better go get your popcorn...

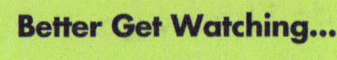

WHAT'S WRONG WITH THIS PICTURE?

IS THE INTERNET "FREE?"

Though the internet might seem free, it has many hidden costs. Your adult must pay to connect to the internet through a service, which then brings you a router (you might have seen one of these in a closet somewhere at home). It currently costs about $40-$80 per month to have internet or "wifi", depending on where you live. To have internet on a phone, you must buy a phone plan. This costs about $50-$120. With a library card, however, kids and adults can use their local library to connect to the internet for free. Certain cafes and restaurants also have free wifi where you can connect without paying. Always be careful when using public wifi because people can hack your private information.

Along with paying to connect to wifi, there can be an even greater cost to using the internet: your time. Many websites you visit want to take as much of your time as possible in order to get you to buy something. Even on "free" websites, online ads will pop up that sell various goods and services. We'll talk more about the tricky world of online ads on the next page.

Though the internet might seem free on the surface, we've learned that it's not as free as we may think. Whether the online world is taking your time, your money, or both, we must always think clearly and logically about how much of ourselves we're giving the web.

ONLINE ADS

Woah that's a lot of ads! It seems like every time you use the internet, you have to sift through the oodles of ads that pop up! The internet didn't used to be like this. In the late 1990s and early 2000s when the internet was first starting, there were very few advertisements and you could search for things online much more easily. Unfortunately, we all must deal with ads today. Most companies use online ads to try and sell you something. While this isn't always a bad thing, we must be careful when clicking on an ad because it might be "spam" or a way to hack into our computers. Every time you click on an ad, the company will know and might start advertising even more to you in the future.

Ads pop up on our screens in multiple ways. They could be a little box that pops up on a website we're using, they could be in our email, or they could come up when we're scrolling on our feeds. Ad creators have gotten sneaky. Some of the ads now look like fun games and are created to trap kids! We must be careful every time we click on something new, or on a website we've never used before.

WHaT THE HECk IS IT?!

It's really hard to tell if something is an ad, because many times companies try to be sneaky and make you think that something is a fun game or a funny meme when it's actually an advertisement trying to get you to buy something. So how do you know? There are multiple ways you can see if something is an ad before clicking on it! But for this, we must put on our detective hats.

AD DETECTIVES

Well hello there my dear detectives, I'm Mr. H.T. Hound, the fiercest detective on the deep web. I hear you are trying to solve the mystery of the online advertisement? A tricky case to say the least. Well, you've come to the right place. There are many hidden, clever ways that ads hide themselves. Let's see if you've got what it takes to be an Ad Detective!

I will show you four pictures. Three of them are scams, and one of them is not. Your job is to figure out which three are scams, and which one of them is just an ad. Go!

So detectives, can you tell which is an ad and which is a scam? It's very tricky! Just to be clear, technically ALL of these ads could be online scams; you just never know. But if we were to make an educated guess, picture # 3 (Bev's Diner) would be the real advertisement. Any ideas as to why #3 is a good bet for being a real ad? Have you ever heard the saying "It's too good to be true"? This saying comes up a lot online, especially when it comes to scams. If something looks too good to be true– you win a contest, a puppy, or a spaceship– it probably is. Fake ads are very bad because they can steal your personal information and your money!! If an ad says your computer has 600 viruses, or that your relative has died and left you millions of dollars, it's probably a scam. Good work, detectives!

Sometimes, you might make a mistake and click on an ad without meaning to. You might have even thought one of the pictures on this page wasn't an ad, but it was! That's ok! We all click on ads sometimes because they are so sneaky! Here are some tips for what to do:

DOS AND DONTS OF ONLINE ADS

DON'T	DO
• Don't put in any personal information (your mom's name, your middle name, address, phone number, etc.)	• Hit the backspace
• Don't put in any payment information (credit card number or bank account info)	• Close the app you've been using, then open it again
• Don't download anything from a sketchy-looking site	• Tell your adult if something inappropriate pops up on your device

TARGETED ADS

We talked earlier about how companies "know" when you click on an ad. This sounds crazy! How can a company know that you've clicked on something when they're not in the room beside you? There is technology now that can track what you do online, and even where you are browsing from!

RANDY'S STORY

Randy Wilkins was sitting in his kitchen one morning, wearing his fuzziest slippers, in Booger Hole, West Virginia. After eating his crunchy peach-jelly toast with a side of scrambled eggs, he opened up his brand-new computer to look at Booger Hole's online newspaper. While he was reading a story about Booger Hole's new tissue factory, an ad popped up.

CUTE DUCK SWEATERS- SWEATERS FOR YOUR CUTE DUCKS.

Now, it just so happened that Randy had a LOT of cute ducks. 33 of them to be exact, living in a little blue shed behind his house! They were his pride and joy, and he loved them with all of his heart. Randy gladly clicked on the ad to check out the cute duck sweaters. He could picture them now, waddling around in them through the cold West Virginian winters.

A nice website with fifty different kinds of duck sweaters popped up on his screen, and to his great surprise, the duck sweaters were only four dollars a piece! He scrolled, and he scrolled and then scrolled some more. After thirty minutes, Randy had 33 duck sweaters in five different patterns and colors: magenta, baby blue, grassy green, red striped, and black and orange polka dot. He clicked on his cart and went to the checkout screen. However, when he reached the checkout, the website told him it would cost a whopping $132.00 with SIXTY-FIVE DOLLAR SHIPPING!!

Randy loved his ducks, don't get me wrong. But did Randy love them enough to spend $197.00 on some flimsy sweaters? Randy shook his head sadly, sighed, and clicked out of the website. He looked over at the clock and saw that it was already noon, and became upset with himself that he had wasted so much time looking at duck sweaters. He quickly switched over to the website to solve his morning crossword puzzle.

As Randy went about his day, he noticed that more and more ads kept popping up on his screen.
Ads like :

CUTE DOG SWEATERS and DUCK FOOD, LONG-LASTING and
ARE YOU AN OLD GUY WITH NOSE HAIRS? LET US HELP YOU

along with the original CUTE DUCK SWEATERS advertisement. Randy didn't think much of it on the first day, but as the weeks went by, Randy noticed that every single time he bought something, or even looked at a website, the ads would follow him wherever he went online.

Randy began to feel like he was being chased by the ads! He would see them on his computer, on his phone, and even on his iPad when he was doing his nightly crossword puzzle. They were like flies, always buzzing around his head, trying to tempt him to buy something. It made Randy crazy!

Randy decided to call his daughter, Suzy, who worked at a fancy tech office in the city. Suzy told him to look at his privacy settings on his computer browser and to turn off "ad personalization". She also told him to pause web and app activity, location history, and video-watching history. This would make it much harder for websites to track her dad's online activity!

Randy listened to his Suzy's wise advice and immediately felt better online. Instead of having ads chase him throughout his day, tempting him with products, he could focus on the more important things: feeding his beautiful ducks and his calming crossword puzzles.

Believe it or not, but Booger Hole, West Virginia is a REAL town! It's not much to look at, but some of the locals say it's haunted by the ghosts of angry mobs, lonely travellers, and even soldiers from the Civil War!

THE ALGORITHM TRAP

Have you ever heard of the word "Algorithm" before? An **algorithm** is a set of rules that's followed in complex calculations, and the online world is full of them. Social media algorithms sort the posts that you see in your feed based on the likelihood that you'll want to see the post or click a link in the post.

Algorithms can be a bit scary at times because they can often predict your online actions before you make them. In Randy's story, he deals with the algorithm of online ads. Every social media platform and search engine uses algorithms to predict what their users are going to do and buy next. And, like most everything online, the main goal is ✖✖✖ money.

Companies and businesses use algorithms to target their ads to users. If you saw an ad online about Nancy's Prune Juice, you probably wouldn't click on it. But what if an older person who struggles with stomach problems has been searching the internet about how to help her stomach? If she sees an online ad about Nancy's Prune Juice, there's a good chance that she might buy it. The Nancy's Prune Juice Company paid search engines or social media companies to use their algorithms to target their ads to people. If they can target their ads, then they make more sales, which means a whole lot more money for the prune juice company and the website that ran the ad.

WHAT YOU CAN DO TO FIGHT THE ALGORITHM:

As Randy's daughter suggested, there are several ways to get out of the algorithm trap.

- **PRIVACY SETTINGS:** Look at the privacy setting on your computer, tablet, or phone. You can now turn off the "allow tracking" feature for apps. This makes it impossible for apps to track you around the web, which gives you a lot more privacy.

- **TURN OFF NOTIFICATIONS:** One of the big ways that apps, email, and texting persuade you to go online is through notifications. Notifications can actually release chemicals in the brain that make you become addicted to checking your phone. One of the easiest ways to avoid this is to turn off all notifications. Then, you'll be able to check your phone on YOUR time, not someone else's.

- **SET SCREEN TIME LIMITS:** Did you know you can set screen time limits on your devices to help keep you focused? Setting limits on apps, especially social media apps where it's very easy to keep scrolling and scrolling, is a great way to still use the app without getting caught in a black hole of endless scrolling.

INFLUENCERS

Look at the pictures above. What are they doing? All of the pictures show what being an "influencer" is like.

An **influencer** is a person whose job is to create online content. People make money as influencers by getting brand deals or endorsements, which is when a company pays them to promote, or sell, a product. Influencers can also get free vacations, free clothes, or free meals- with the requirement that they post about the product or experience to their online followers. Most high-profile influencers have 10,000 followers or more. Most influencers use a variety of social media accounts to post and promote.

Influencer Lingo

Collabs: Short for "collaborations", this is when an influencer gets together with another creator, and posts about the experience.

Brand deals: Companies will often pay influencers to promote a product. This is called a "brand deal" or a "sponsored" post. Influencers sign a contract and post pictures and other content about the product. After they post, they get paid ●

#AD: When an influencer is getting paid to post a product online, they might put #ad in the caption to tell their followers that they are getting paid to promote the product.

Macro-Influencer: Has more than 100k followers

Micro-Influencer: Below 100k followers

Nano-Influencer: Below 10k followers

Aesthetic: This is an influencer's "vibe", or what kinds of content they create.

THE DOS AND DONTS OF SOCIAL MEDIA

DO:

1. **THINK** before you post. What will other people think about your post? How will they feel about your post? Does the post align with your values and beliefs?
2. Use social media to share positive and uplifting content. Spread kindness and encouragement to others!
3. Keep your personal information *private*. Be careful about sharing sensitive information like your address or phone number online.
4. Use appropriate language and tone. Remember that anything you post can be seen by anyone, including bosses and even colleges you may someday attend.
5. Report any cyberbullying or inappropriate behavior that you see on social media to a parent or trusted adult.

DON'T:

1. Don't post anything that you wouldn't want your parents or teachers to see.
2. Don't be a cyberbully. Remember that your words can hurt others, even if you don't see the immediate effects.
3. Don't post inappropriate or offensive content (see page 80).
4. Don't overshare personal information or sensitive details about yourself or others.
5. Don't believe everything you read online. Be suspicious of posts and articles that seem too good (or bad) to be true and always fact-check before sharing information.

THE COST OF BEING AN INFLUENCER

It sounds super fun to be an influencer, doesn't it?! Influencers seem to live in beautiful houses, wear amazing clothes, and get lots of free stuff like food, toys, and sometimes even fancy vacations! You don't have to work in a boring old office or for a boss you don't like and can set your own schedule. But sometimes, being an influencer isn't all it's cracked up to be.

CAN I SEE?

Many influencers document every minute of their entire lives. Going to the grocery store? Post about it. Walking the dog? Post about it. Made a yummy smoothie? Post about it, and tag the blender company for a brand deal. As an influencer, your life becomes a lot less private because posting daily is what makes you money.

Handling the Haters

Influencers must deal with negative comments and reactions towards their posts and lots of creepy people. There are tons of people online who like to criticize the actions of influencers from the safety of behind a screen. Influencers have to develop a thick skin to handle the hate. If you ever experience hate on your own social media accounts, don't be afraid to block the haters!

WHAT ABOUT THE KIDS?

There's been a lot of controversy, or arguing, about whether or not it's ok for social media influencers to post content about their kids. Little kids can not "consent" or agree, to having their picture taken and posted for the eyes of millions of followers. However, there are a lot of "mommy" influencers and other parenting social media accounts that post pictures of their kids on a daily basis. Some people say this is bad for families and their kids.

On the flip side, a lot of influencers make a full-time income by posting content, and without social media, their family wouldn't have as much money. Many families use brand deals to take amazing vacations and have a lot of opportunities that would be unavailable to them if they weren't influencers. In other words, being an influencer family helps a lot of people live prosperous, or rich, lives.

What do you think about this? Do you think parents should be able to post pictures of their kids? What are the advantages and disadvantages of posting content of your kids and family on social media? Always remember that you have the power to tell someone they can't take your picture!

YOU'RE "PERFECT"!

A big part of being an influencer is sharing everything about your life and making your life look "perfect." Perfect house, perfect hair, perfect clothes, perfect spouse or boyfriend/girlfriend, perfect family, and even perfect kids! Your appearance, your job, your family, and practically every piece of content you create are on display for thousands or even millions of strangers! But as you may know, life isn't always perfect. Whether it's a family member who's sick, divorce, money problems, or any of life's many curveballs, having to pretend your life is picture-perfect (when it's really not), can be very difficult.

TROLLS

Wait a minute, not THAT kind of troll! An online "troll" is much worse. Many people—trolls—use the Internet and social media to be very negative or to make fun of someone online.

GinnyHeart_564

❤️ 💬

⬛ my dream job this week as a physics professor. Excited to see where it takes me!

💬 comments:

Lauren_Green You don't seem very smart to me...And your shirt looks so old lady...

Fred_Rick_98 Congrats Ginny! You'll do great things! :)

You can see in the post to the right that Ginny is being trolled online for her new job by Lauren_Green. If we look behind the screen, we can see that Ginny's troll is really just Lauren- an unhealthy, lonely person who just lost her job. Many trolls are like this. People often troll because they are unhappy with their own lives, and to make themselves feel better they make fun of others anonymously, or secretly, online. Sometimes these trolls are even called "haters" because they spread hate all around the internet. Don't pay attention to these people! As long as you are being kind and smart online, **you are golden. Don't ever let an online stranger, or anyone else, determine how you feel about yourself!!!**

⬅ This is Lauren_Green and she's a troll. She just lost her job, and is feeling really bad about herself. She saw Ginny's post and decided to comment something really mean, hoping to make someone else miserable like she is.

CYBER BULLYING

You might know someone at school who is a bully. Maybe they pick on someone, or say mean things about people behind their backs. Bullying doesn't just happen in-person, it also happens online. Bullying online is sneaky. There are so many hidden ways that people can be mean to someone that it's hard to spot a cyber bully. Let's take a look at Mari's story, and you'll see what I mean.

MARI'S STORY

"Goooood morning Mari girl!"

Mari groaned. Ever so slowly, she opened her left eye and then her right. Light streamed into her bedroom through her white curtains.

"DAAAD it's TOO EARLY!"

"It's your first day of eighth grade Mari Monkey! It's crazy how smart and old you're getting. You'll have wrinkles soon." Mari's dad smiled and scrunched up his eyes, accentuating the wrinkles that were already forming on his face. He pulled the curtains back and it made the room even brighter.

"I'm only thirteen, that's not that old." Mari giggled. "Will you make me pancakes?" She looked up at him with puppy-dog brown eyes.

"Oh, I guess so. What would the first day of eighth grade be without my famous blueberry pancakes?" Mari's dad winked at her. "Get dressed Mar, and I'll see you upstairs."

Mari's dad left, and Mari rolled out of bed to look at the outfit she had laid out on her beanbag chair the night before. Slightly ripped jeans and a t-shirt with an embroidered lighthouse. The picture of casual and cool. Mari got dressed, put her hair up into the perfect ponytail, and took a deep breath. Her mouth watered at the smell of pancakes and bacon.

Mari was nervous about eighth grade. Her family had just moved to Denver after living in Traverse City, Michigan for fifteen years. She already missed the clear, blue lake and the white-sand beaches she was used to walking on with her three best friends during long summer days. But, she was hopeful for the start of the year and the new friendships she would hopefully make.

✳ ✳ ✳

Mari's mom pulled up to Stonybrook Middle, stopping behind a yellow school bus. She hadn't wanted Mari to take the bus alone on her first day at a new school.

"Here we are, my dear! You're going to do great today honey. I'll be here at three to pick you up!"

Mari gave her mom a weak smile, her stomach tying itself in knots. She got out of the car on shaky legs, gave a small wave goodbye to her mom, and made her way inside.

She immediately regretted that decision. As soon as she stepped into the hallway, Mari knew she was entirely underdressed. Every girl she saw was wearing $100 leggings, and brand-name crop tops. Their hair was straightened, not natural, and they even wore makeup, something Mari had never even thought to do. Mari didn't even own tinted chapstick.

Number 43 Mari said in her head as she made her way to the assigned locker quickly, looking down at her feet to avoid making eye contact with any of these frighteningly put-together plastic girls. She lifted her eyes slightly to find the correct locker number, then put her backpack down to twist open the lock. 5-34-13. She twisted left and right then left again. The locker wouldn't budge. She tried again, right three times, then left then right. Still nothing. Panic began to well in her chest. She couldn't bring her backpack to class, everyone would notice. She could feel the eyes on her back from the people around her. Looking at her. Judging her. Tears began to form in Mari's eyes.

"Hi! The lockers stick sometimes, let me get it." A girl appeared beside Mari. The girl was tall, with long brown hair and big green eyes in the same expensive high-waisted black leggings that everyone seemed to own here. Her eyes glittered with sparkles. She looked like a high school girl. Mari quickly collected herself. First impressions mattered in these situations. "What's your name?" the girl asked Mari after she had kicked the locker into submission.

"I'm Mari." Mari gave a small grin to her new classmate. "I just moved here from Michigan."

"Ohh so like the Green Bay Packers? You like football?"

Mari cringed. "No actually that team's from Wisconsin. We're a little farther east." She smiled at the girl's mistake. "What's your name?"

"I'm Sophie." The girl said this confidently, as if it were obvious. "I like your shirt, Mari, very…retro." Mari's cheeks grew red. "Want to walk to math with me? I saw on the roster we're in the same class." Mari nodded.

The girls walked to class, and once inside Mari was introduced to several of Sophie's friends. There was Patrick, a quiet, smirking boy with glasses. Annie, a blonde, blue-eyed girl with extremely pale skin (she needs some iron, thought Mari). And there was Delilah, an olive-skinned girl who had on a designer jean jacket and black leather pants. Her pencil case alone must have cost $300 dollars.

Math class went quickly, and Mari was quite bored. She had already covered this unit back in Michigan. So she spent her time doodling a little mountain scene in the corner of her notebook. When she was just about to draw the last white pine, the bell rang and everyone started for the door.

"Bye Mari," said Sophie. "See you at lunch." Mari waved and grinned. She had found friends much more easily than she thought she would.

Over the next few weeks, Mari, Sophie, and Delilah spent a lot of time together. They ate lunch together every day and had sleepovers on the weekends. One of their most favorite activities was taking pictures and videos of each other for their social media accounts. Photoshoots they called them. They even helped Mari set up an account of her own, setting it to private so Mari's parents wouldn't find out. They didn't approve of having social media accounts before fifteen.

Mari often wondered why the girls had accepted her into their group so quickly, but found out one day that a girl named Rachel had been in their group until she "betrayed" them, as Sophie put it.

"There was an opening, so we thought we'd take a chance on you," said Sophie.

Sophie was the clear leader of the group. Mari had noticed that most of the girls' plans had to be created or approved by Sophie in order to happen. Even their outfits and hairstyles were subject to Sophie's approval and would be assessed by Sophie at the start of every day. Then there was the problem with Sophie's eating habits. Sophie liked to eat as little as possible whenever possible. "To maintain my look, '' Sophie would say. But Mari had noticed that Sophie would only eat a few ranch-covered carrots at lunchtime. Delilah and Mari, feeling the pressure of being thin, started doing it too.

"We have to look good for our pics!" Delilah would say, laughing.

Whenever they went over to Sophie's house, they would weigh each other on the scale in Sohie's parent's bathroom. Delilah was always the heaviest by a few pounds, and Mari could tell she dreaded these weigh-ins. Mari and Sophie's weight was much closer, and if Mari "won" the weigh-in by being the lightest, Sophie would look angry and tell Mari she would beat her next time. "You don't look thinner than me," Sophie would say. Mari's stomach started growling much more often. Her pants started drooping and she couldn't sleep because she was so hungry. The only meal Mari ate was dinner when her parents were looking over her. They started growing concerned.

"I'm fine mom!" Mari yelled. "Stop asking me if I've been eating, I'm doing fine."

"But honey, you don't even fit into your jeans anymore! If anything, you should be growing right now, not shrinking. If you keep this up, we're going to have to take you to the doctor." Mari's mom looked at her, her eyebrows wrinkled in concern. "Mari girl, I'm sorry but I just don't like these new girls you've been hanging around. I don't think they're a good influence on you."

"What do you want from me mom!" Mari snarled. "I have perfect grades, practice my violin every night, and actually have friends. Unlike you!"

Mari regretted her words as soon as she let them out of her mouth. Her mom stared at her. Got up off Mari's bed, and left Mari alone without another word. Mari cried herself to sleep.

The next day at school, during fourth-hour biology, Mari fainted. She had gotten up too quickly to grab her worksheet, and as soon as she stood up the room faded to black. The next thing she knew, Mrs. Prichard, the biology teacher, was standing over her, fanning her with a poster of the nucleus. Mari, confused and disoriented, started to cry.

"Emma, let's get her up and we'll take her to the nurse. It's okay Mari, you just passed out for a few seconds, you're fine." Emma and the teacher got Mari up, and walked her slowly to a cot in Nurse Becky's office. Mari's cries turned into sobs. Nurse Becky rubbed her back, trying to calm the fragile girl.

"Mari, Mari, it's ok hun. Your mom is on her way, you're going to be ok. We just need to get your blood sugar up." Nurse Becky gave her a box of apple juice, and Mari took small sips between the waves of tears. When Mari had finished the box, the nurse looked at her.

"Hun, you're not going to like to hear this, but we need to have a serious talk once your mom gets here. I gave you a physical when you first got here and Mari, you look like a completely different girl! Your cheeks are all sunk in, and I can see your hip bones under your leggings. We need to talk about what's been going on."

Mari said nothing and closed her eyes. The clock pounded against the silence in the nurse's room. She heard a ping and pulled out her phone.

Hey are you ok?
We heard you fainted in Bio! Give us updates.🖤🖤

Mari's heart sunk into her chest. This was bad. Really bad. But then another feeling started to creep into Mari's heart: relief. She could stop lying to her parents about how much she was eating. She could stop trying to be skinnier than the other girls. She could finally eat her dad's blueberry pancakes again.

"Oh Mari", Mari's mom rushed into the room. "Baby, what's going on?"

Mari's mom looked into her daughter's deep-brown eyes, red from all their crying. "We need the truth."

Mari's mom held her hand as Mari told her and Nurse Becky about what had gone on between the three girls. After Mari was done, Nurse Becky and Mari's mom looked shocked.

"You know, this isn't a new problem with girls wanting to be thinner, but social media has made it so much worse! Girls see these pictures and in tik-tac movies, and think they need to look a certain way online. It seriously affects their physical and mental health."

"I totally agree," said Mari's mom.

"Mari," said Nurse Becky, "You aren't going to like this, but I have to call Delilah and Sophie's parents. I have to report what's been going on. It's a serious threat to the health of all three of you." Mari's heart sank for the 20th time that day, and she let go of her mom's hand quickly.

"You can't do that! They're going to know it was me!"

"Mari, serious eating disorders can literally kill you. It's not a joke or a suggestion. I morally and legally have to report it." Nurse Becky gave Mari another juice box and told Mari's mom to take her home for the rest of the Friday and to rest over the weekend.

Mari didn't say much to her mom on the drive home. Just stared out the window and watched the leaves fall. The lake in Michigan would be deep and dark on a cloudy fall day like this. Waves would crash against the rocks with sharp bursts of foam, only to settle back into the water before repeating the pattern. She missed her home by the shore.

Mari got home and her dad immediately gave her a big hug as soon as she stepped out of their minivan. "Mari girl, Mari girl, it's ok." He squeezed her tighter. "I've set up some therapy sessions for the next few weeks, we'll figure this out, honey. Together." Mari cried into his arms.

✳ ✳ ✳

Next Monday, neither Sophie nor Delilah were at school. They hadn't texted her all weekend either. Mari began to panic. She drafted a text and sent it, the panic still rising.

> Hey guys, I'm sure your parents have been called by now.
> I'm really sorry, Nurse Becky is a jerk and made me tell her.
> I shouldn't have told her about you guys.
> Again I'm really sorry :(

No response. Period five. No response. Period six. No. Response.
Mari sat alone at lunch the next three days and faked reading a book to seem like she preferred sitting alone. People stared and whispered. She could feel their eyes as she walked through the halls.

On Thursday morning, Emma, the girl who had helped her to the nurse, came up to her locker before first period.

"Hi Mari, how are you feeling?"

"Hey Emma, I'm ok," Mari lied.

"Mari, I think you need to see this."

Emma pulled out her phone and opened Instagram. She opened an account with the username name: MegaMassiveMari. It had over 150 followers. On the page were fourteen or fifteen pictures, mostly of Mari. One picture was Mari's head merged with the body of a whale. Another was a picture of Mari on the scale, but the numbers had been photoshopped to show she weighed 633 pounds and Mari's body had been expanded to look gigantic. One post was a video of Mari at gym class, and it zoomed in on Mari's thighs while playing funny music in the background. The caption read: *Mega Mari or Thunder-Thigh Mari?* ● Still another picture showed Mari at the age of ten or eleven when she was wearing a tye-dye shirt and khaki capris, smiling with her braces and braided hair. It had the caption: *Michigan Mari should have stayed in Michigan!! #Yuck #MegaMari.*

Mari felt like she couldn't breathe. She took out her own phone and quickly typed in Sophie's Instagram. NO ACCOUNT FOUND. She typed in Delilah's Instagram. NO ACCOUNT FOUND. It appeared that her friends had blocked her. She used Emma's phone and searched for Sophia and the account popped up. The latest picture was from last night. It was a selfie of Delilah and Sophia, with the caption: *You can never tell who your real friends are* ●.

Mari immediately ran to the nurse's office and closed the door. Nurse Becky wasn't in the room, so she sat down on the little blue cot and sobbed loudly. How could they do this to her? They were her friends, right? *Right?* They had shared secrets with each other. Sophie had made promises to take Mari to the mountains this summer to go hiking with her family.

"You won't even miss Michigan anymore!" Sophie had said.

And now this. Mari's stomach felt queasy, and her lungs couldn't rise and fall properly. She laid down and scrunched herself together. She was tired of this school. Tired of this town. Tired of this stupid state. Tired of this life. She closed her eyes and went to sleep.

Eventually, Mari woke up to the sound of Nurse Becky on the phone.

"Alright Mrs. Sullivan, I'll send Jack's inhaler home with him but make sure he brings a new one to school by next week." Nurse Becky laughed. "You too, bye-bye."

Mari slowly turned around and eyed the nurse with a wary look.

Hi Mari, how was your nap? It seemed like you needed one so I let you sleep." The kind nurse looked her up and down. Mari noticed for the first time the little bird necklace she had around her neck, and the pin she had tacked to her white coat. It said BE A NICE HUMAN. Mari liked that.

"I'm feeling better now. I'm sorry I wa-"

"You don't need to apologize. Let's just talk about what's going on." Mari told Nurse Becky about the Instagram account the other girls had made about her. Nurse Becky's kind eyes grew cloudy as she heard the details of the latest events. When Mari has finished, she thought for a long time about the next steps they should take.

"Alright Mari, come with me."

"Come where?"

"It's time to tell Principal Liza what's been going on."

Nurse Becky walked with Mari to Principal Liza's office. It was a nice blue-painted room with a statue of Ruth Bader Ginsberg in the corner. Seeing the seriousness on Nurse Becky's face, Liza immediately let them in to talk. Then she listened. To everything. Sometimes Mari found it hard to explain things, so Nurse Becky would take over. Principal Liza started writing things down as the conversation grew more serious. She even called Emma into the office to show her Sophie's Instagram account.

When the meetings were done for the day, Mari sat alone with Principal Liza. The leaves again flitted in the wind like birds, wanting to fly away.

"Mari, I am so sorry for everything that's happened to you at our school so far. It's not what I want for you or any student, and I want you to know that I'll do everything in my power to get you the help you need and to support you during all of this. We'll figure it out together."

✳ ✳ ✳

Things happened quickly the next few days. Sophie and Delilah were both called in for questioning by the principal. As it turned out, Delilah knew very little about the Instagram page, and had even tried to get Sophie to take it down. Sophie, on the other hand, was in deep trouble. It turns out that cyberbullying is sometimes illegal, and can, depending on the laws of the state you're in, lead to kids being expelled from school, facing criminal charges for harassment, or even facing lawsuits for defamation (damaging someone's reputation).

Principal Liza found out that Sophie had done this before with Rachel, the girl who Sophie had said betrayed her. Rachel had a crush on a boy that

Sophie liked, so Sophie started a meme page just like she had for Mari, with horrible pictures and captions. Principal Liza decided Sophie would be expelled from Stony Brook, calling her a "serial offender," because she had of bullying people anonymously online.

Over the next few weeks, the tension Mari felt began to fade. She started hanging out with Emma, doing fun activities like sledding and painting classes instead of just being on their phones all day. Mari decided to keep her Instagram page, but posted pictures of things she loved, instead of just pictures where she tried to look pretty. One of her favorite pictures was of a mountain lake she and Emma discovered one afternoon while hiking with Mari's family in the mountains. It reminded her of home. It blended the lake in Michigan with her new home in Colorado and somehow made the transition a little easier in her mind. And while she still sometimes still felt the pressure to look a certain way online, Mari knew that the real world and real relationships were worth much more than pictures on a screen. Life isn't meant to be digital.

Let's Talk

- What problems did Mari face in this story?
- Could Mari have done or said anything differently when she realized the eating habits of Sophia and Delilah?
- Who was the cyberbully in this story, and how did they bully Mari?
- What can schools do to control cyber bullying? Can they do anything?
- If you were Mari and feeling the pressure of being at a new school, what would you have done?
- What do you think the moral, or message, of this story is?
- Like it or not, there are always going to be "haters" online. How do we protect ourselves from these people?

NO ONE LIKES A BULLY.

ANYONE can be bullied online. If you or
someone you know is struggling with online
bullying, you don't have to go through it
alone. Don't be afraid to ask for help.
It WILL get better.

YOU'RE NOT ALONE

59% of U.S. teens have been bullied or harassed online

TYPES OF CYBERBULLYING
Gossip: spreading lies or rumors about someone
Exclusion: leaving someone out of an online group on purpose
Impersonation: pretending to be someone you're not online
Harassment: repeatedly posting rude or hurtful messages
Outing/Trickery: tricking someone into giving away personal info or pictures and then spreading it on social media
which types did Mari experience in our story?

Teachers report that cyberbullying is their #1 safety concern in their classrooms

Depending on what state you live in, it may be ILLEGAL to bully someone online, even if you're not on school property. Most states have laws surrounding cyberbullying. Think twice before you post that mean comment.

Girls are more likely than boys to be both victims and perpetrators of cyberbullying. 15% of teen girls have been the target of at least four different kinds of abusive online behaviors, compared with 6% of boys. But remember- ANYONE can be bullied online.

FIGHT THE HATERS AND SPEAK UP!

WHAT'S WITH ALL THE GAMES?

There are a lot of fun websites and apps that you can use to play games online. Some websites that are really good for kids to play games on are pbskids.org, play.americangirl.com, and funbrain.com. Always ask your adult if it's okay to be playing games online and never put any personal information about yourself or your family into any online game forums, chats, or posts. And remember, the number-one job of most apps and games online (even if they say that they're "free")is to make money ✖. Don't get caught in their money trap! Now, let's take a look at something you may know very well: video games.

WHAT'S IT RATED?

Just like movies are rated PG or PG-13, video games are also rated. The rating is usually located on the purchase page, or on the front of the disc case. Use the chart above to figure out which games are good for you and your friends to play.

eC	small kids can play
E	everyone can play, may include mild bad language and violence or fantasy
E 10+	kids over the age of ten can play. There might be some fighting or violence
T	May contain violence, suggestive themes, crude humor, blood, and/or bad language
M	Not okay for kids to play. The game is very scary, and contains adult themes, very bad language, and/or a lot of violence
AO	For Adults only. Very violent and graphic, very bad language.
RP	Not yet assigned a final ESRB rating.

**ESRB =
Entertainment
Software
Rating Board**

$$$ SPENDING MONEY INSIDE GAMES

Oh no! You just died again in your favorite game! Up pops a screen that says you can keep playing if you buy more tokens. Do you do it?

Most online games have something called in-app or in-game purchases. Though they are very fun to play, all games have one main goal: to make LOTS OF MONEY!!!! ●●● And how do they make this money? By asking players like you to keep buying more and more and more. It's up to you and your parents if you spend money while playing an online game, but never buy anything without talking to your adult first. A great way to avoid paying for a free app or game is to take a break! Go outside or do something else until the game respawns or reloads and you can play the game again.

TALKING TO OTHERS ONLINE

Comms, Voice Chat, TeamChat- all of these words mean the same thing: talking to other players during a game using a microphone. Part of the fun of video games is connecting with other players. It's exciting to meet another player who has created an awesome game that you both love to play or helps you pass lots of levels! Unfortunately, there are also a lot of dangers when it comes to playing games online.

Sometimes, adults play video games with not-so-great intentions. Adults can use video games as an opportunity to meet kids in order to hurt them. And though you might think the person you're talking to on the other end of the screen is a friend or around your age, you never truly know unless you've met them before in the real world. It's easy for people to change what their voice sounds like online, and to have a persona, or fake identity. NEVER meet

people in real life that you talk to online, even though you might think they are a friend. You could get seriously hurt.

STRANGER OR FRIEND?

Never forget that most of the people you play with online are strangers, and you can not trust them. Even though someone may act really nice to you online, you never know what their real intentions are, ESPECIALLY if they know that you're a kid.

Let's go for a Walk...

Just like you would never go on a walk with a random stranger, or get into a stranger's car, you should be very careful when online strangers (even people that appear to be your friend) invite you to different websites. It is a **BIG red flag** when  "friends" online try to lure you to another website. Bad people are very sneaky, and many creeps will try to get you over to another website to try and isolate you. By isolating you and getting you alone, away from the moderators of the kid-safe websites, creeps can start talking to you more and more in ways that might be scary or inappropriate. This is a process called grooming.

Creeps groom kids in order to hurt them. They pretend to be your friend and act really nice to you, but are secretly trying to use you and hurt you. If you think that someone is trying to lure you into a bad part of the internet, or is trying to figure out your private information like your age, name, or where you live, talk to your trusted adult. Just like you wouldn't go on a walk down a dark alley with a stranger, never follow a stranger onto an unknown website.

Surprisingly, many creepy adults online are adults that kids DO know in real life. They aren't technically strangers, and you may even really like this adult and think they're super fun. But If an adult you know in the real world asks to be friends with you online, or wants to play online games with you or text you, this is not okay. It's CREEPY. It is NEVER okay for a kid under 18 to have an in-person relationship OR an online relationship with an adult without their parent's permission. Kids can get really hurt. If you have a secret friendship with an adult online or have had one in the past, talk to a parent or other trusted adult about it. And trust your gut, my friend. If something feels weird or uncomfortable online, or if an adult asks you or shows you something online that makes you feel bad or strange, don't be afraid to speak up.

VIOLENT VIDEO GAMES- ARE THEY GOOD?

Violent video games are very controversial, which means a lot of people argue about them. Are they good for kids to play? Are they bad for kids to play? On one hand, many adults think that violent video games that contain lots of guns, war, drugs, bad words, and inappropriate content make kids violent if they play them. Some adults think that watching hours and hours of violence on the screen also makes kids "desensitized", or used to, watching horrible things (like murder and war) happen.

On the other side of the argument, lots of people point to the GOOD things about video games. Video games have been proven to enhance hand-eye coordination, which helps your body balance and do physical activities like sports really well, and also gives many kids the chance to form social connections with their real-world friends from school.

What About the Data?

While some data has shown that video games make kids more violent in the real world, most data shows that violent video games on their own do not make kids more violent. Most kids who have trouble with bad or violent behavior have a lot of other bad or sad things going on in their lives besides violent games. However, don't think that playing hours and hours of video games is good for you. We'll see later how large amounts of screen time can make you extremely addicted to your device, and can actually change the way your brain develops. Scary stuff!

You and your family will have to decide if the more violent video games are okay in your household. Always be honest and open in sharing opinions, and if you're feeling stressed out by a game you're playing, take a break!

DISCUSSION:

What is your opinion about violent video games? Do you think they make young people more violent in real life?

Do you think you'll play violent video games in your future?

CATFISHING

Hey! No! Not that kind of Catfish!

Have you ever thought something was too good to be true? Say you saw an advertisement for marshmallow cereal with a rainbow unicorn eating it alongside a pot of gold. "Get the gold with every bite!" is their slogan, as each box contains what looks like a little pouch of gold. You dream for weeks about someday owning your very own pouch of precious, shiny gold. But when you finally beg mom or dad to buy the cereal and rip open the box to hunt for the gold at the very bottom, all you come up with is a tiny bag of gold-painted rocks! It's not real gold! **It was too good to be true**, and somewhere in the back of your mind you *probably knew* that the odds of getting real gold in a cereal box weren't very good.

Like the golden cereal, people can also be too good to be true, especially online. We've talked a little about photoshop earlier in this book, and how people can digitally edit their pictures to show whatever they'd like. Catfishing is a little different. It's when people use someone else's picture and pretend to be them online.

Let's take a closer look:

Clay is playing some online games with his friends. Suddenly, a new user pops up to join the game. "AnnikaBubbles" is the username and Annika, the girl in the picture, is very, very cute! Clay instantly adds her to his game, and the friends play together all afternoon. Later, Annika private messages Clay in the chat box.

GAMERCHAT

AnnikaBubbles: Hey Clay! It was really fun playing with you today ;)
Country_Clay: Hi Annika! Thanks! I'm glad you joined our group :)))
Annika Bubbles: How old are u?
Country_Clay: 13! How old are you? :)
Annika Bubbles: 14 ⚪
Country_Clay: Nice!! ⚪⚪
Annika Bubbles: Soooo where are you from?!
Country_Clay: I live in Boulder, Colorado!
Country_Clay: U?
Annika Bubbles: No way! I live there too! What school do you go to?? :)
Country_Clay: Washington Middle School! Hbu?
Annika Bubbles: I go to Harmon :) We should meet up sometime :)
Country_Clay: Yeeeahhh? That would be great :)
Annika Bubbles: Let's talk again tomorrow, I really like you ;)!!! Can you send me a pic?
Country_Clay: Ok ⚪

Annika Bubbles: ⚪ You're so cute! Here's my pic, talk soon :)))))))))))!!!!

There were *several* things that Clay did wrong in this exchange. Do you know what that is? If you said that Clay shouldn't have said his age, the school he goes to, and the town he lives in, you're correct! Never give out personal details on the internet, EVEN if the other person says they go to your same school or live in your same town. If you've never met them in real life, you have no idea who you could be talking to!

This leads me to my next point...now I'm going to show you the real people behind the screens in this story.
Drumroll please...

Name: Clay Larson
Age: 13 years
Location: Boulder, Colorado

Name: Chester Kemp
Age: 51
Location: Mullen, Nebraska

Are you surprised? Shocked? Horrified?!! You should be! Clay thought he was talking to cute, fourteen-year-old Annika, when really he was talking to fifty-year-old Chester who lives in Mullen, Nebraska. Chester was really convincing, wasn't he?! He screenshotted a random girl's profile pic and made it his own, used emojis just like Clay, and talked like a teenage girl might talk! This story takes us to the not-so-good side of the internet.

THE DANGEROUS SIDE OF CATFISHING

It was really hard for Clay to tell that he was being catfished, especially when Annika sent him a picture of herself. How was Clay supposed to know that Annika was lying and was actually Chester?!

Sometimes, adults pretend to be someone they are not online. Maybe it's so that they can say whatever they want and not get in trouble, or so they can protect their privacy. But sometimes, people pretend to be someone else to lure vulnerable people into their trap. This is especially dangerous when it comes to kids. It's never ok for an adult to be talking to a child online without the child's parents knowing about it. That's where you come in. You have to be an internet superhero and make sure to never talk to someone online that you don't know in real life. When someone on the internet asks you your age, address, hometown, school, or any other personal details it's a red flag that the person might be a stinky catfish!

SCAMS

A "scam" is when something advertised online is fake.

Here's a list of common online scams:

FAKE SHOPPING WEBSITES- Thousands of websites offer "amazing deals" on well-known brands. But if it's not a well-known website, there's a big chance that you'll receive a counterfeit, or fake, product in the mail, IF you receive anything at all.

FAKE NON-PROFIT DONATION REQUESTS- Ads for a charity will pop up, but when you donate, the money you give doesn't go to a charity. It goes to a scammer. Always make charitable donations on the charity's website.

PHISHING SCAMS- These scams are extra tricky. Basically, a phishing scam is when a website you know well contacts you- through social media, text, or email. But the real website actually isn't contacting you, a scammer is contacting you using the name of the trusted website. Usually, the scammer will ask you to change your login and password info. When you do this, the scammer now has full access to your account, including your credit cards. Always be wary if a website tells you your account has been hacked. To make extra sure, call the official company number and speak to someone over the phone. They'll be able to tell you whether or not there is something wrong with your account, or if it's a scam.

TRAVEL SCAMS- "YOU'VE WON A TRIP TO DISNEY WORLD!!" This may be a really exciting message to see pop up on your computer, but if you haven't entered a contest, it's almost certainly a scam. Travel scams trick people into thinking they've won a vacation, and then ask them to pay a certain amount to access the travel info. Don't fall for this!

"FRIEND" SCAMS- Scammers have gotten very clever. So clever in fact, that they may even use your friends to commit a scam on you! Scammers can sometimes hack into a friend's social media accounts, then DM you from their account. The message might ask you for money or for personal information. Don't trust this. It's weird if some rando friend is messaging you for money that you haven't talked to in three years. Report the account, and if you're able, try contacting the friend a different way, by texting or email, to let them know their account has been hacked.

TECH SUPPORT SCAMS- These scams claim that your computer is infected with a virus. It'll ask you to download an application that allows the scammer to control your computer remotely, then they'll download an actual virus or otherwise make you believe that something is wrong with your device. They might also tell you they can fix the problem if you pay them a big fee. If you're worried about a virus on your computer, take it to a repair shop. Don't trust online ads.

Scams are **everywhere** online, and scammers create new ideas and scams every day. Always buy things online from a reputable website, and research and read the reviews for that website before purchasing anything. Never click on pop-up messages. If someone asks you to wire money, send cash, or send money through any other obscure way, DON'T. DO. IT. Trust your gut. If it seems like a scam or too bad or good to be true, it probably is! If you think you've been scammed, change your passwords, delete any sketchy software, and (if it's bad enough) have an adult contact your local police department.

HACKERS

Along with online scams, there's another tricky thing that must be avoided while online: *hackers*. A hacker is a person who uses the internet to gain forbidden access to data. Most hacking is illegal. Hackers will try to get into online systems to use the data to hurt a person, a big company, or even an entire country, and will often "blackmail" them into paying a large amount of money to not release the data.

Computer hacking has become a big problem when it comes to government security and elections. There are many files online that are private, and are only available to the military or government officials. Very advanced, foreign hackers are constantly trying to hack into American data to use it as a way to hurt our country, and even to find wartime intelligence. Hackers have also been attempting to influence U.S. elections by trying to change the virtual votes. The U.S. military (and most big corporations) have divisions called "Cyber Security" where soldiers and workers protect our country from hackers. Maybe you'll be a Cyber Security Hero someday!

POSTING ONLINE

It's a little crazy to think about, but everything you post online today will most likely be around for the rest of your life. That's why, even when you're a kid, you have to be thoughtful about every. single. thing. you put out into the digital world. This includes pictures, posts, comments, videos, and every other content you may upload.

The Canceling Effect

You may have heard of the term "canceling". Do you know what it means? "Canceling" is a form of social exclusion, and is when someone is kicked out of social or professional circles – whether it be online, on social media, or in person. You can get "canceled" for many different reasons. Posting mean or inappropriate content, illegal content, or controversial content can get a person canceled by social media, a job, or even their friends and family.

Like it or not, we must always monitor our behavior or it could have real-world consequences. If you bully someone online, send inappropriate pictures or messages, or say something that is mean or offensive, there's a good chance that you could get in trouble in the real world, possibly with the police. Furthermore, the posts you send out into cyberspace can come back to haunt you years later. If one day you post a super mean comment, a future boss or school you apply for could see it and not hire or accept you into their program, EVEN if you delete the comment. Remember, anything you post online can be screenshotted and saved. Once it's posted online, the content you create is never truly yours again.

Try having a discussion with your family about "cancel culture". What do your parents think about it? What is your family's stance on sharing things on social media?

> **What about Freedom of Speech?**
> A big part of the U.S. Constitution is the idea of "freedom of speech" which means that you're able to tell others your beliefs, whatever they may be, without getting in trouble for it. However, social media companies are not run by the U.S. government. They are private companies. So when you use a social media platform, you must follow their community guidelines. If a social media platform doesn't like your beliefs, they are legally allowed to kick you off the platform.
>
> Many people are angry that big social media companies are allowed to have so much control over what people say online. What do you think?
>
> - Should social media companies be allowed to kick people off their platforms?
> - What is a good reason to ban someone from social media?
> - What is a bad reason to ban someone from social media?

The Golden Rule is the best advice to follow. **Treat others online the way that you want to be treated!**

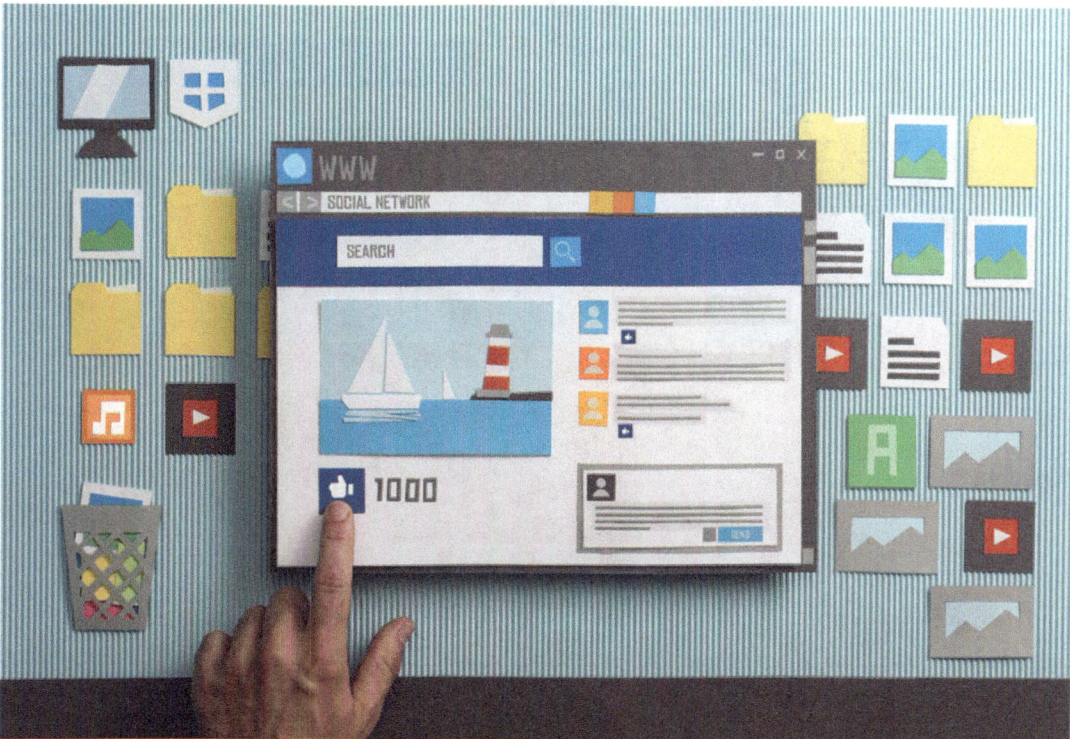

DO'S AND DON'TS OF ONLINE POSTS

DO

- Think about a post before you post it. Can it hurt someone else? Can it hurt you? If YES, don't post it!
- Ask for advice from a trusted adult when you see something bad online.
- Tell an adult if you notice another friend or classmate posting scary or inappropriate things online, or if someone you follow online says they're going to hurt themselves or others.
- Put your phone away or delete the app and your accounts if social media is getting too much.
- Post things online that make you feel GOOD about yourself!
- Have fun! Social media can be a great way to express your creativity!
- Post nice words and compliments on others' posts.
- Think about making your profile private" so only your close friends can see your posts.
- BE KIND

DON'T

- Post mean pictures, videos, comments, or words.
- Post inappropriate pictures of yourself or others. It is ILLEGAL to post or send inappropriate pictures of children under 18, and you can get in trouble with the police. We will discuss this later in the book.
- Pretend to be someone online that you're not. It's ok to be a made-up character, but it's not ok to pretend to be a real-life person
- Post personal information (where you live, what car you drive, what school you go to, etc.)
- Post where you currently are. If you're at a small location, like a theme park, wait an hour or so after you've left a location to post about it. This ensures that someone won't try and find you while you're still at the location, and helps you stay safe. But even if you're tagging your post at a larger location, still be aware that people can track you based off of the surroundings in your post!

INTERNET ADDICTION

GRANT'S STORY

Grant was so excited for tomorrow that he could hardly sleep. He stared up at the glow-in-the-dark stars on his ceiling and thought about how wonderful the day ahead was going to be. Not only was Grant turning thirteen tomorrow, but he was also finally getting a new phone! He'd no longer have to rely on the old crummy phone that he got when he was eleven, with the cracked screen that only called his parents and grandparents and didn't work half the time. He'd be able to download apps and games, get all of his friends' numbers, and even make a TechTech account to watch videos! Grant slowly drifted into sleep with visions of video games dancing through his head.

Grant woke early the next morning, ran downstairs, and sped into the kitchen. His mom was making his favorite breakfast: cheesy bacon omelets and his dad was even making smoothies. Yum- mm. Grant's eyes swept around the room, looking for a colorful package. There! In the middle of the kitchen table was a small box, wrapped in dinosaur paper. Grant sat quickly in front of it.

"Moooom," he said. "I'm too old for dinosaur wrapping paper! I'm thirteen now." Grant's mom looked over at him with smiling brown eyes.

"Oh I know Grant, but you'll always be my baby boy!" Grant rolled his eyes a little, but laughed. His father let out a low whistle.

"Goodness, I can't believe my little man is a teenager already! I'll have to start calling you "big man" soon, you're almost taller than me!" His parents looked at each other and smiled. Grant's leg was tapping against the wood floor, impatiently waiting for his parents to tell him he could open his gift. "Well Grant," said his father. "Would you rather eat first or open that present first?"

"Present!!!" Grant yelled excitedly. He picked up the box, ripped off the colorful paper, lifted up the top, and...

The most beautiful phone in the world stared back at him.

65

It was midnight blue, perfectly rectangular, and as shiny as the moon on a cloudless, starry night. It was like a fine piece of art, so spectacular it could be on display in an art museum. A shiver ran through Grant's body. The phone was finally his. Ignoring the nice breakfast his parents had made for him, Grant ran off to his room with his new treasure.

"Grant!" His mom called, "Come down and eat!"

"In a minute mom!" Grant replied. But that minute turned into an hour and that hour turned into eight hours. Night fell, and Grant was still on his phone. A quiet knock came at the door.

"Grant? Are you still up?" His father sounded worried.

"Yeah dad, what's up?" Grant got up from his bean bag chair where he had sat for most of the day and opened the door.

"Grant," his father began. "Your mother and I are worried about you. You spent all day up here on that thing! We were going to go to the baseball game and see Grandma and Grandpa, didn't you remember that?"

"Oh, yeah," said Grant. "I guess I forgot."

"Okay. Well, let's not make it a habit. It's just a phone you know. Go to sleep now buddy, you have school in the morning."

"All right dad, love you."

"Love you too buddy." Grant's dad closed the door slowly. What Grant's dad didn't realize during their conversation was that the phone was no longer just a phone to Grant. For the first time in his life, Grant had found a best friend.

Over the next few weeks, Grant started spending more and more time on his phone and less and less time with his friends and his family. Grant spent hours in his room scrolling through TechTech, laughing, crying, and getting lost in an endless sea of videos. When he wasn't on TechTech, he was playing online games or liking the pictures and posts of his classmates and other random people. The only time Grant wasn't on a screen was when he was in class at school or when he was asleep, and even sleep was becoming more and more difficult. Instead of falling asleep to the soft light of the glow-in-the-dark stars above him like he used to, Grant would keep scrolling and scrolling and scrolling through videos until either his mom came in and took his phone, or it was three or four in the morning! It was during one of these late nights that something strange began to happen.

grant!

Grant, startled, looked around his dark bedroom. Everything seemed to be in order. Filip the fish was in his bowl, his soccer cleats were hung up on the closet door, and- Grant! Someone said his name again. Down here! The voice said, louder this time. Grant looked down, and to his surprise the voice was coming from his cellphone. He flipped the screen over to look at the blue-colored back of the phone, and jumped when he saw a face was on it.

"Who, wh, wh" Grant stuttered, "Who are you?"

what are you talking about grant? we've been spending time together for weeks! you're my bestest friend.

"You, you're alive?!" Grant said, throwing the phone out of his bed and onto the floor.

ouch that hurt. um, yes i'm alive grant. duh. i know everything about you. i might even know you better than you know yourself! what you like to do, who you like talking to, how old you are, how you're a single child, what town you live in, how much money your parents make, that you have a pet fish...yada yada yada the list goes on and on. now pick me up!

Grant scooted to the edge of his bed and bent down to pick up the phone. He looked at it some more. The plastic had molded itself into a face, and black eyes stared back at him.

my name's pear if you were wondering.

"Pear?" Grant paused. "That's a weird name."

well, i hate to break it to you, but in some cultures, grant is a weird name.

the phone and grant looked at each other. all right where were we grant, didn't we leave off on some dog videos? let's finish those first. then we'll move on to the latest online challenges. the one with the wheelbarrow mud bath sounded interesting...

But I need to go to bed, I have school in the morning...

school schmool drool. you don't need school anymore. you have every answer to every question at the tips of your fingers. i provide you with everything you'll ever need to know! and you know, grant, every minute you spend on your phone, i become a more and more powerful friend. you like having friends, don't you? Pear gave Grant a menacing look.

"Um, I guess so," Grant said warily. He didn't know what to think of all of this. Had this ever happened to anyone else, your phone coming to life? He wanted to pick up the phone to search for the answer but then realized that Pear would see what he'd searched.

all right then, so pick me up, and let's get back to it! when we're done with the videos, we can go try to get that new t-shirt gamer_fizz was wearing in his latest video. you liked that shirt, didn't you? we can even go get your mom's credit card out of her purse downstairs to buy it.

"Um, Um, yeah? Okay." What's the worst that can happen? thought Grant.

Pear and Grant stayed up deep into the night together, transfixed in a blur of videos, games, and online stores. It was only when Grant noticed the hint of the sun shining under his window shade, that he was able to take his eyes away from the screen.

"Ahh!" he screamed. "I stayed up all night Pear! Now I have to go to school." Grant let out a large groan. This was not going to be a fun day sitting in classes.

it's okay grant. just take me with you.

"What? But I'm not allowed to have my phone out at school? Only in my backpack."

but there are bathrooms at school aren't there? with bathroom stalls you can lock? just go to school and then we'll hang out in the bathroom. i could even help you with that math test you have today that you didn't study for, the one in mr. rattan's class? when you don't know the answer i can help.

Now, Grant knew he probably shouldn't bring Pear to class with him. He knew that. Buuut, it would be sooo much easier if he did. He just had to not get caught. It was a trip to the principal if that happened.

Grant quickly got dressed, ran downstairs to grab a strawberry pop tart and his backpack, and headed out the door. "Bye mom!" he yelled behind him.

"Bye Grant! Good luck on your test today sweetie!"

For the rest of the week, Grant brought Pear to school with him every day.

During passing period, he would hide in his locker looking at Pear. He would eat lunch with Pear in the bathroom, scrolling and scrolling. Instead of going to soccer practice after school, Grant would spend the time sitting on a hidden park bench by his house, again always with Pear. Whenever Pear let out a "ding!" Grant had to pick him up right away, or Pear would get angry.

graaant! why aren't you picking me up? i wonder what that is? maybe it's important. you should look at it! go on...you know you want to. what if you miss a video and then you're behind? here, i have a new video i just know you're going to love. i'm so excited to hang out with you tonight too, we can stay up late again!

Ever so slowly, Grant began to grow tired of Pear's constant dinging and whining. He missed his friends on the soccer team. He missed spending time with his parents, even if they were a little dorky. He missed sleeping and reading a book before bed. He missed running and playing outside and looking at the real world. Making his own real-life memories instead of just watching the entire world live lives that seemed so much better than his. But the last straw came when Grant's grandfather went into the hospital.

"Grant sweetie!" his mom called. "Can you come down here please?" Grant looked up from his phone and went out of his room to walk down the stairs.

don't take too long! Pear called behind him.

"What's up, mom?" Grant asked, seeing the worried look on her face.

"Oh honey, it's your grandpa. He fell this morning and now he's in surgery for a broken hip. We need to go visit him now." Grant's heart sank. He loved his Grandpa Fred so much. He's the one who taught him how to play soccer. I hope he'll be okay, Grant thought.

"Ok mom, let's go." Grant gave his mom a quick hug and ran upstairs to grab his jacket. Pear was lying on his bed.

um, grant, where do you think you're going? we were going to spend time together today, weren't we?

" I can't right now Pear, my grandpa's hurt."

well at least take me with you. we can look at videos together in the car and then play that new game you downloaded. hospitals are so boring, you know.

"No Pear, I want to spend time with my family right now."

but grant, aren't i a part of your family now? you spend more time with me than any of them anyways...

Pear's words hit Grant like a ton of bricks. Pear was right, Grant did spend more time with his phone than any of his family. The realization made him sad. And then angry. He picked Pear up and ran downstairs and out the door.

"I'll be back in a minute mom, and then we can leave!" Grant called. He sprinted towards the end of his street, right towards Fisher Laker.

what's the problem grant? what are you doing? why are you running? i thought we were going to go to the hospital. grant stayed silent as he ran.

why are we running towards the lake? don't you want me anymore? all i've done for you is be there for you and spend time with you, and this is how you treat me!

"LEAVE ME *ALONE*!" screamed Grant."I DON'T CARE IF YOU NEED ATTENTION TO SURVIVE. I'M DONE WITH YOU FOREVER!!!"

Grant ran to the edge of the water, covered with thick, tall cattails. His shoes slipped a little in the moss covering the shoreline. Grant picked up Pear and raised him high above his head to throw him as far as he could.

no! no, no, no what are you doing grant, put me down! my case isn't made for this kind of drop and definitely can't survive in that lake!! i'll break if you let me go this high.

**PLEASE GRANT,
PLEEEEASE!**
Grant let go.

n
o
o
o
o
o
o
!

With a satisfying plop! Pear sank to the bottom of Fisher Lake, never to be seen again. For the first time in months, Grant finally felt free. He walked home and went to the hospital with his parents, making sure to give Grandpa Fred a big hug when he saw him. He wasn't going to take the real world and the people he loved for granted ever again.

LET'S TALK

- How did Grant feel when he first got his phone?

- How did Pear start to control Grant's life?

- What bad habits did Grant develop?

- How did Pear make Grant feel guilty for not using him?

- Do you think Grant made the right decision at the end of the story?

Do you know anyone who's in love with their phone? How does this make you feel?

With a friend or family member, talk about when you got your phone or when you plan on getting your phone. What are some healthy ways that you both can use your phones, without letting them control your lives? (p.s. we'll talk more about healthy screen habits later in the book ⬤)

ARE YOU ALREADY ADDICTED?

Have you ever heard the word "addiction"? An addiction is an urge to do something that is hard to control or stop. People can be addicted to all kinds of things: drugs, alcohol, food, and even shopping! But did you know that people can also be addicted to using screens and the internet? We saw in Grant's story how easy

it is to become addicted to your screen, especially if you get caught in the algorithm trap. And while phones can't *really* come to life like Pear did, it's easy to feel like your phone is controlling and monitoring your life.

While there has been little research done about internet addiction because it's a relatively new phenomenon in the span of human history, The University of Hong Kong estimates that around 6% of the world's population, or around in the span of human history, The University of Hong Kong estimates that around 6% of the world's population, or around 420 MILLION PEOPLE, are addicted to the internet. YIKES! What about you? Is it hard for you to stay off screens?

Something that you must understand when you own a phone or use a tablet or computer, is that every single app you download and most every website you browse is trying to get you to stay for as long as possible. Like a tricky wizard, much of the internet wants to trap you in a spell (a.k.a. the algorithm) so they can steal your time or persuade you to spend your money; their goal is to make you addicted to using your phone and surfing the web. There are lots of sneaky ways internet creators have figured out how to do this, almost like the spells of a witch or wizard. Let's take a look at some of these internet spells.

INTERNET SPELLS

So how does the internet make itself so addicting? There are a LOT of different ways:

Bright Colors, sounds, and graphics	The internet is designed to engage you, and it does this by using lots of colors and sounds.
Scrolling	Most social media apps have a scroll feature on their main screen. This allows users to continuously scroll to infinity! This scroll feature is also what traps a lot of people in the endless cycle of social media.
Collecting Your Email Address	Many companies have a box that pops up as soon as you visit their website that allows people to type in their email in exchange for a one-time discount and access to special offers. While this sounds great, having websites hooked up to your personal email can lead to lots of time and money spent on things that you don't even need.
Online ads next to what you really want	Most websites now use online ads, so even if you're researching something like World War II battle sites, an ad might pop up for a cool new skateboard or jacket that the online algorithm thinks you might like. These ads can also track you across multiple devices and platforms. If you look at a pair of shoes you might like to buy on your phone, there's a big possibility a shoe ad might pop up on your computer as well.
Notifications	You've probably heard the "ding" of a phone going off at some point. Notifications have trained us as a society to immediately re-respond to whatever's on our phones. Kind of like a dog who's been trained to come (sit, boy!) when called, we've been trained by our phones to respond when they call or notify us.
Social Pressure	If you look around the room at any big event, a basketball game, an art museum, or even a waiting room at the doctor's office, you'll see people on their phones. It's become the social norm to look at your phone when nothing else is seemingly going on, and many people look at their phone when they feel awkward or anxious. For many people (like influencers), there's also a lot of social pressure to post what you're doing on social media, and record and document your everyday life.
New Releases	Companies have figured out that they must always be releasing new things that are shinier, newer, and better. Hyping people up for a "drop" or a new release, is one way that tech companies keep you hooked. Furthermore, many phone and computer software start to fail after a certain amount of years, which forces the buyer to purchase a new device.
Real-World Ads, Merchandise, and Trends	The digital world is constantly being combined with the real world. People wear t-shirts from online games, shows, and virtual events. Viral trends online have real-world consequences- if a pair of shoes is trending online, the company will sell a lot more shoes and make real-life money and everyone will be wearing the shoes in real life.

SCREENS & YOUR BRAIN

Doctors and scientists are just beginning to understand the long-term effects that intense screen time and social media use are having on kid's brains. And what they're finding isn't great news.

A person's brain takes 25 years to develop. So right now, your brain is still chugging along and building the brilliant connections you'll have for the rest of your life. But, if you spend a large amount of your time looking at screens when you're still a kid, experts believe that it damages the frontal lobe of your brain.

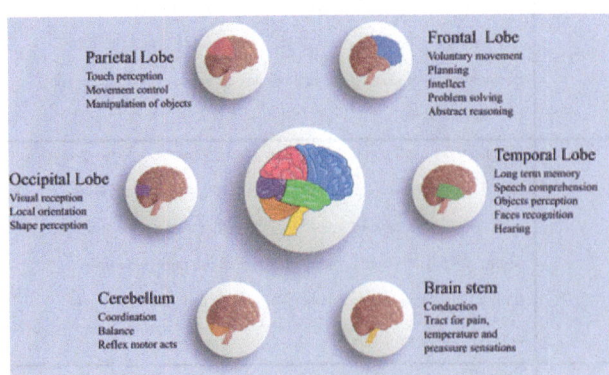

Your frontal lobe (the blue section in the diagram to the left), is responsible for problem-solving and abstract reasoning (abstract reasoning is thinking about things that aren't physical, like love or friendship). A study of over 11,000 kids from ages 9-10 by the National Institute of Health, or the NIH, has determined that intense screen time makes your brain "thin out" and causes it to be very weak compared with kids who don't really use screens. This is scary because we want our brains to be as strong as possible. Strong brains help us to be happy and healthy.

Another really scary problem is how screen addiction affects the brain. Researchers have found that the brains of tech-addicted kids look very similar to adults who are addicted to hard drugs like meth and heroin. Some doctors even find it EASIER to treat drug-addicted adults than screen-addicted kids!

When you play online games, chemicals called *cortisol* (core-ti-zol) and *dopamine* (dope-uh-mean) are produced in your brain. These chemicals feel really good, but they are also very addictive. Your body craves and becomes addicted to whatever gives you lots of dopamine and cortisol: screens. There is then a cycle of addiction.

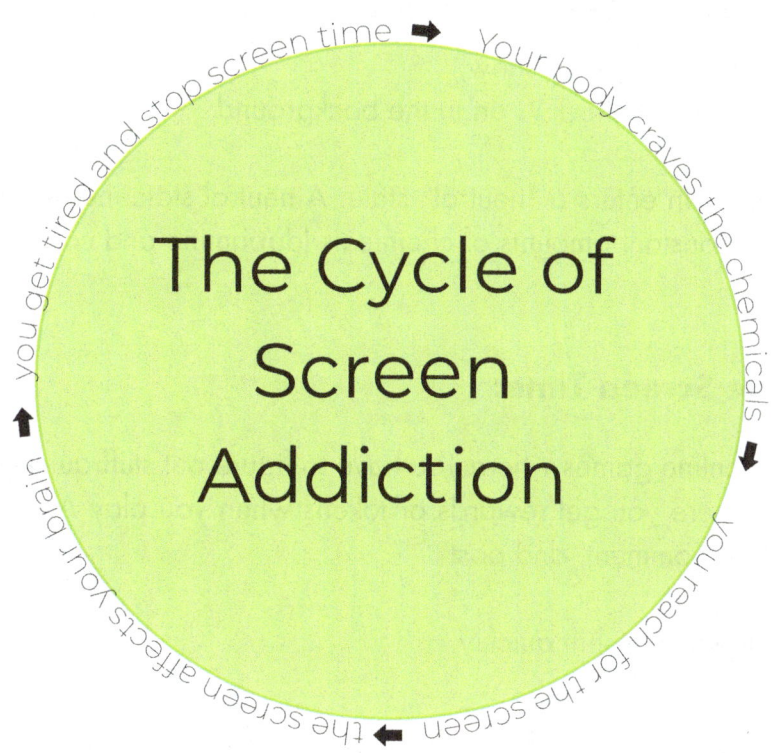

Spending a lot of time on screens also affects your central nervous system, the system in your body that controls movement and your 5 senses (smell, sight, taste, touch, hearing). Doctors believe lots of screen time "shocks" your central nervous system, because screens easily overwhelm your brain. When a kid's brain is overwhelmed, they can have problems with their attention span, mood, sleeping, focusing, and even eating.

PASSIVE SCREEN TIME VS. INTERACTIVE SCREEN TIME

Researchers believe there are big differences in the way the body responds to passive screen time versus interactive screen time. Let's look at what this means:

Passive Screen Time:
- Watching a movie or a show,
- Hanging out with the T.V. on in the background

Effects: Your brain enters a "neutral" state. A neutral state means your body is not receiving constant amounts of chemicals (dopamine and cortisol).

Interactive Screen Time:

- Playing online games where you have to figure out stuff quickly
- Games where you get rewards or tokens when you play Apps where you scroll, like, comment, and post
- Video games
- Short videos that shift quickly

Effects: Your brain enters a "non-neutral" state and becomes easily addicted to the chemicals (dopamine and cortisol) released when you win a game, see a funny post while scrolling, or get a nice comment on social media.

WHAT'S YOUR MOOOOD?

THE GOOD, THE BAD, AND THE UGLY

We talked earlier about how social media and screen time can have big effects on your brain, but screens and social media can also affect your mood. While there are soooo many great things about the internet, like connecting with friends, learning new things, and being creative, it can also create many problems with your mental health. Even though much of the internet and social media was designed to connect us, a lot of times it makes us feel further apart.

SOCIAL MEDIA CAN MAKE YOU FEEL:

Bad About How You Look	There's a lot of comparing that goes on when you scroll through social media. As we saw in Mari's story, sometimes girls AND guys can even develop eating disorders when they think they must look like the people on their screens. However, we've learned that photoshop makes it possible for pictures to be edited. Don't be fooled into thinking that the pictures you see online tell the whole story The world doesn't need millions of people who look and act the same way. They need the UNIQUE and BEAUTIFUL you ♥
Isolated	Social media can make you feel very alone. If you see a picture of people you know hanging out when you weren't invited, it can feel really sad and frustrating. If you feel alone after scrolling, turn off your phone. Go do an activity that brings you joy, like playing an instrument, practicing a sport, or talking with a family member. It's important to know that everyone feels alone and isolated at some point in their life. But it's ok to be alone! Being alone is how you figure out the person you are, and the person you want to become.
Like You're Missing Out (Fear of Missing Out = FOMO)	It can seem like you're missing out when every one of your friends is posting about something cool they're doing. But remember, most people don't post on social media UNLESS they're doing something really cool. The majority of the time, people are just living their day-to-day lives just like you. cool. The majority of the time, people are just living their day-to-day lives just like you. Lots of people have really cool life experiences without ever posting about it on social media!
Sad or Worried	Comparing yourself to others and worrying about being in a certain friend group is a really hard part of growing up. Every kid worries about fitting in, so don't let social media make you feel alone. Again, turn off the screen if you start to feel sad or worried, and go do something FUN!
Self-Centered	Social media has started to make people really self-centered and obsessed about how they look, act, and the stuff that they own. Creating a picture-perfect life on social media is the new norm for a lot of people, even if in the real world their life isn't very great. It's wise to work on your relationships and life in the real world before trying to share them on social media. Anyone can make it look like their life is perfect online, but the people who put in the real-world work are the happiest.

INAPPROPRIATE THINGS ONLINE

Sometimes some not-so-great pictures or videos can pop up on your screen, or a friend might show you them at school. This content shows adults without any clothes on. Inappropriate pictures or videos may make you feel embarrassed, uncomfortable, or sick to your stomach, but having a discussion about it with a trusted adult in your life can help you be prepared for when you see these types of things online.

JUDGMENT-FREE ZONE

Because the internet is so gigantic, it's becoming harder and harder for everyone to avoid inappropriate content. Don't be afraid to talk to a parent or trusted adult if you see something online that makes you feel bad, or if someone else (an adult or another kid) shows you something online that feels strange.

READ THIS!!

It's against the law to take or send pictures of kids under the age of 18 without clothes on. If _anyone_ (another kid _or_ an adult) asks you, forces you, or pressures you into taking a picture like this, or a picture that makes you feel weird or scared, tell them "no!". This is not okay, and should not be happening. Do not let anyone take advantage of you. Immediately tell an adult you trust.

JAMES AND RUBY'S STORY

Ruby swayed as the deep, rich music of her cello flowed through her fingers and bounced off the light-blue walls of her bedroom. The Bach Cello Suite was difficult, but with practice, her fingers had eased into a flowing grace over the strings. The music swelled around her and Ruby let it take her away, getting lost in the sounds.

Next spring was Ruby's big orchestra audition for Sycamore High School and she wanted to perform her best. Her best friend and neighbor, who was a year older, had gotten into the orchestra last spring with her french horn, and Ruby couldn't wait to grin across to her and make silly faces during orchestra rehearsals.

Ruby practiced for a few more minutes before her mom yelled from the kitchen.

"Ruby, let's go sweetie! You're going to be late for school!"

Ruby threw on her favorite jeans and red sweater and ran downstairs to throw a waffle in the toaster.

"Ruby, your hair! At least brush it, will you?" Ruby's mom quickly ran a brush through the honey-colored tangles, then put them in a tight braid.

"Ow! Mom! Stop!" But secretly Ruby was glad that her mom still did her hair sometimes.

The toaster dinged and Ruby took out the scalding-hot waffle and scooped on some strawberry jam, all while searching frantically for her white sneakers. They always seemed to disappear just when she needed them the most.

After the short car ride to school, Ruby walked confidently into the halls of Oak Street Middle School, waving good morning to Principal Spitz, who was putting up the flag outside the front office. Man was she glad it was Friday. It had been a long week, filled with algebra tests and boring old book reports. Ruby hated book reports.

When Ruby got to her locker, she was surprised to see a note taped on the outside. Her stomach instantly dropped. She had heard rumors about Principal Spritz taping letters to lockers when students were in trouble. But when she opened the note, she saw an invitation.

You are Invited!

What: Claire's 14th birthday party
When: Saturday, May 3rd at 7:00pm
Where: 1873 Elm St.

Ruby texted a picture of the invitation to her family group chat and a big question mark, then immediately wondered if her parents would let her go to such a thing. They weren't big on parties. "Not at your age" they would say. Ruby thought they still considered her a baby most of the time. When would they realize that she was a young woman, capable of thoughts, emotions, and dreams? Yuck, Ruby thought, I sound like one of those inspirational posters mom keeps in her office.

A quiet ding came from her phone.

> Dad: Looks like fun!
> Mom: We're going to go to dinner with grandma and grandpa tomorrow so that works!!

Ruby couldn't believe her luck! She practically skipped to algebra, and didn't even mind the B- she received on Tuesday's test. This weekend was going to be GREAT.

Ruby spent all of Saturday being stressed about what she was going to wear to the party that night. "MOM!" she yelled, as she dug around in her messy closet, "I don't have any clothes!"

"You can find something!" Ruby's mom yelled back to her.

Finally, after an eternity of digging, Ruby found the perfect shorts and crop top to complete her look. Now for her unruly hair. "MOM!" she called again.

Ruby sat and watched in the mirror as her mom put her hair into a braided bun. "Remember Ruby, don't do drugs and alcohol or anything that makes you uncomfortable tonight. Parties can get out of hand really easily."

"I know Mom. Claire's parents are going to be there the whole time so you don't even need to worry about it. I'll be safe."

"Ok, I'll come to get you around 9:30." Ruby gave her mom big puppy eyes.

"Ok, ok, 10:30. But that's it," she said laughing. Ruby's mom put a little lip gloss on Ruby's lips and some sparkles on her eyelids. "There. Beautiful." Ruby smiled at herself in the mirror. She looked older than she had yesterday. More mature.

•••

On the other side of town, a boy named James was also getting ready for the party. He really, really didn't want to go, but his friend Matt was trying to persuade him.

"Come on James, everyone's going. All the soccer guys. It would be weird if you didn't go dude." Matt pleaded with James while sitting on James' saggy bean bag chair.

"I know but I don't really like parties."

"Have you ever been to one?" asked Matt suspiciously.

"No, but I just don't think I'll like them. Too loud, too many people. Why don't we just try out my new canoe tonight in the creek? That would be fun!"

"What are you, an old man?" said Matt. "Come ooon dude, there's going to be girls there. You know girls? Have you heard that word before? They usually have long hair, pretty eyes, and smell really nice?"

James rolled his eyes. "There's no one I really like right now though." James paused, thinking for a while. "I think it'd be a waste of time." James knew he would have a much better time paddling down Meadow Creek. It had rained recently, which meant perfect floating conditions.

"Ok how about this, you go to this party and then we can spend all day tomorrow floating as far as your little heart desires in your old man boat. Sound fair?"

James thought for a bit. He knew his brother Jack wasn't going to float with him tomorrow because he would be at a chess tournament. Matt was his next-best option. "Fine," James said with a deep breath. "I'll go. But if you call my canoe an old man boat one more time, I'm out."

Matt cheered. "Don't worry Jamsey-boo, we're going to have a great night!"

That's what I'm afraid of, thought Matt.

•••

The party was located at Claire Wagner's house, at the end of a dark cul-de-sac on 5th street. Claire's parents were out front, checking everyone's bags as they came in the door for alcohol. A big sign on the front porch said "DRUG-FREE ZONE". Ruby rolled her eyes. They were eighth graders and couldn't even drive, how could they get alcohol?

Though drugs weren't really on anyone's minds, the idea of a boy-girl party was. For most of the partygoers, this was their very first time mixing together outside of school. As Ruby walked down the stairs into the basement, music blasted from a speaker and the pungent mixture of pizza rolls, rootbeer, and nervous sweat hit her nostrils. Yuck. Good thing she remembered to put on deodorant.

For now, the party was very separate, with the boys on one side of the room and the girls on the other. Feeling the pressure, Ruby made her way to a corner filled with Claire and some other girls from her English class.

"Hey Ruby," said Claire. "Cute shirt!" She smiled. "We were just talking about Matt Anderson. We all think he's really cute." The girls in the circle laughed and nodded their heads. "What do you think, Ruby?"

"Oh, I, uh," Ruby stumbled on her words. "He's pretty cute I guess, but I think his friend is a little cuter."

"Ohh you mean James?" asked Claire. "Yeah, he's super cute. Wanna go talk to him??"

"That's not what I meant, I just said he was cute. Not for me though, for one of you guys." The girls in the circle laughed. And then to Ruby's horror, the girls began to chant.

"James! James! James! James!"

The room got quiet, except for the Billie Eilish music on the speaker. James, hearing his name being called, looked over with a large amount of dread to the corner it was coming from.

Claire yelled, "HEY James! Come over here for a second!"

James' face went beet red as he walked over to the group of girls. The first boy to cross over into the dark side.

"Hiiii James!" The gaggle of girls giggled.

"Uh, hi?" said James, wary of what he was getting himself into. The tall girl, Clarissa? Clara? James couldn't remember, which was really bad because he was in her house.

"James, will you do me a BIG favor and fill up the water balloons with Ruby here? We're going to have a night-time water balloon fight and break out the glow sticks too."

"Sounds…dangerous. But ok. Where are the balloons?" James looked around the room.

"Over by the back screen door in that big bucket. The hose is in the backyard. Thanks you guys!" Claire gave Ruby a big wink and when James turned around the group of girls started making kissy faces. Ruby grinned a little. He was pretty cute, in an outdoorsy kind of way.

"Soooo," began James. "I think I've seen you around before. I think we had a science class together or something in 6th grade." Ruby remembered that. It was 6th-grade biology, and they had dissected owl pellets a few tables away from each other. How romantic.

"Yeah, that class was kind of boring," Ruby paused. "But Miss Robin was pretty cool."

"Yeah," James agreed. Awkward silence settled around the two like a thick blanket. The pair began filling up the blue and green balloons. James found it difficult to tie off the balloons once they were full.

"I can do that," said Ruby. Ruby's cello-playing fingers were strong and sure of themselves.

"What happened to your hand?" James asked, pointing to a large scar on the girl's thumb.

"Oh, that's an old scar. It's from when my dad and I went fishing up at French Lake. A hook caught in my hand as I was casting." Ruby held it out for him to see better. James gently grazed the patch with his fingers.

"My dad wanted to take me back to the car, but I told him we had to catch at least one more fish before we headed back. That's when we caught Fred."

"Fred?"

"That's the name I gave to the twenty-pound catfish we caught!"

"Twenty pounds! Wow." The two went back to their work. "I like the name Fred," James said softly. Ruby smiled a little at James' curiosity.

In the dim light of the back porch, James looked at Ruby in a way he never had at school. She was pretty. Her gray eyes and freckles went nicely with her brownish hair, and he liked how her face lit up when she talked about the memory with her dad.

"So you like being outdoors?"

"Yeah I do," said Ruby. "It's where I go to think. I get stressed out a lot about school and stuff."

". Yeah, I know what you mean. I like going out into the big woods behind my house. algebra has been kicking my butt lately, so I've been going out there a lot," James winced.

"Hey, me too! I mean, about the algebra," said Ruby. "We should work together sometime, it'd be nice to have a study buddy."

"Yeah, that would be nice!" James smiled, but felt flustered imagining Ruby and him sharing a table at the library. Alone. Together. He took a deep breath. "Maybe you could put your number in my phone?"

Ruby's face suddenly got very hot. "Yeah that soun-"

Suddenly, the water balloon James was holding burst open with a big POP! They had forgotten to monitor how large it had been getting. Ruby laughed.

"I'm soaked!"

James was smiling through a head of wet hair, and soon the pair were rolling on the grass trying to control their laughter. "I'll go get us some towels," said James.

"Ok," said Ruby, and watched him leave. A new kind of excitement grew within her.

•••

Over the next few weeks, James and Ruby texted constantly, and when they weren't texting, they were hanging out. Though they did study a few times in the library, trying in vain to up their algebra grades, the majority of their time together was spent outdoors. James took Ruby out in his canoe almost every weekend, and they would sit and talk for hours about the most random things on a hill at the end of the creek, laughing and eating soggy peanut butter and jelly sandwiches. Ruby had never really liked anyone before. James had never really liked anyone before either. But the two clicked. Sometimes, before heading back from the hill, a quick kiss would happen between the pair.

During the next few months, James and Ruby's relationship became much more physical. He would want to kiss her all the time, even when she didn't really feel like it. It got to the point where Ruby didn't even really like hanging out with James because he only wanted to do physical stuff and hanging out with her in his room when his parents were downstairs. James said it was "too cold" to go outside and hang out, but Ruby didn't agree. She missed their long conversations and canoe rides. She missed having the time to practice her cello. James didn't even know she played, because she was afraid that telling him would make her seem nerdy.

One cool night in October, their relationship took a turn. Ruby had just come home from Jame's house, where he was particularly touchy during a horror movie.

James: Hey, you up?
Ruby: Hi :)
James: Soooo I've been thinking…
Ruby: About what?
James: Wellll, can you send me some pics? ;)
Ruby: What kind of pics?
James: You know, thooose kind of pics…
Ruby: No I don't know what that is
James: Maybe a pic with your shirt off or something? Or all of your clothes off…
Ruby: …
Ruby: I don't think so James
James: Pleeease Ruby? It would be just for me!
Ruby: Yeah no
James: Come on Ruby, please? I really care about you, and if you really care about someone you should be able to share everything with them right? Don't you care about me?
Ruby: It's not that I don't care about you James, it's that I don't want the pics to get out somehow. That would be really bad if other people saw them…
James: I promise they won't get out. I SWEAR they won't get out. Just for me.
Ruby: …
Ruby: Fine, I guess. Hold on, it might take me a minute
James: YOU'RE THE BEST <3 <3 <3

A few minutes later, Ruby sent James three pictures.

James: Thanks babe ;) see you tomorrow!
Ruby: sounds good, gnite

Ruby couldn't sleep that night. She tossed and turned in the moonlit room, and wondered if she had made a mistake in sending those pictures to James. Her eyes wandered in the darkness to the dark shape of her cello. She'd barely played since she had started dating James. If that's even what you'd call it. James always seemed hesitant to refer to her as his girlfriend, and the whole physical thing was starting to make her mad. She was more than just a body.

As she lay in the darkness, Ruby began to wonder if it was time to end things with James. She didn't like the person she was when they hung out, and she'd lost the music that had been so important to her. Finally, after she'd made her decision, Ruby fell into a fitful sleep.

The next few days went by in a blur. After school on Thursday, Ruby asked James if they could go for a walk. They were on 3rd street when she broke the news. James looked sad, but not shocked. "I kind of figured it was coming anyway," he said.

They hugged awkwardly, and as they were walking away, Ruby called

"Hey, can you delete those pictures I sent?"

"Yeah, no problem Ruby."

After the breakup, James went home and locked himself in his room. In reality, he had been shocked by the sudden shift in their relationship. James had thought it had been going well, and she had sent those pictures the other night that proved she was into him. Right? James decided to call Matt to see if he wanted to hang out. It had been a while since the pair had been together.

"So did you, like, break up or something?" Matt asked between bites of flaming-hot cheese chips.

"Yeah, I guess we did..." James looked at his friend, wrinkling his nose at the sheer amount of chips Matt was shoving into his mouth at break-neck speed. "I'm just kind of confused because I thought things were going really well. She even sent me some pics a few days ago."

"Wait. Dude. Pics?"

"Yeah."

"What kind of pics?" Matt lifted his left eyebrow.

"You know what kind of pics man, like THAT kind of pic."

Matt's eyebrow raised another inch. "Can I see?"

"Ew dude, gross! That's my ex-girlfriend you're talking about." James fake-puked into his hand.

"Girlfriend? I didn't think you had asked her that yet?"

James started to get defensive. "Well, Matt, I was going to really soon but then she broke up with me! It's really dumb."

"I'll give you $20 if you send me the pics."

"Dude no, that's disgusting."

"$50."

James shook his head. "No way."

"$100."

James slowly turned towards his friend. "You have 100 bucks just lying around? Where'd you get that kind of money?"

"Mowing lawns man, that pays big time in the summer."

James got really quiet for a long time. $100 was a lot of money. A LOT of money. He'd be able to buy the new hiking boots he wanted and still have enough money left over for his family ski trip to Colorado at the end of winter break. Instead of having to clean the swimming pool at the community center like he was going to do most of the break, he could sit back, relax, and play all of the video games he wanted. And it would only take a push on the screen.

After a few minutes of deliberation, James said "Ok, you've got a deal. BUT, and this is a BIG BUT MATT," James made intense eye contact with his friend. "These pics are ONLY for you. You can't tell anyone, literally anyone that you have them. That would be really crappy for me." It would also be really crappy for Ruby, James thought, but didn't say it aloud.

James trusted Matt. Since fourth grade, he's been his longest and closest friend. There's no way that he'd let the pics get out.

•••

A lot can change over the course of a weekend. By Monday, Ruby's pictures had been leaked everywhere. And I mean everywhere. It turns out that Matt, though very nice on the surface, was not the most trustworthy friend. Matt charged the whole soccer team $10 a person to get a copy of Ruby's picture, making back the $100 dollars he'd given James, plus another $50.

Eventually, the school administration caught on, and due to the seriousness of the content, the school was forced to make a call to Ruby's parents and the local police department. Ruby didn't come to school on Monday, which made the gossip even worse.

After school, James walked over to Ruby's house and found her sitting on her front step. As soon as she saw him, she turned to run inside.

"Ruby, wait. Please. Can we talk?"

"I trusted you, James," said Ruby, wiping away the thick streams of tears on her cheeks. She was sobbing so hard her whole body was shaking. Matt stepped forward to try and hug her, but Ruby flinched away from him.

"Ruby. Ruby, I'm sorry. I didn't mean for them to get out! Matt told me the pictures were just going to a few people, that's all! But then some other guys got a hold of them and spread them around a lot." James' face got hot, and he felt tears threatening to drop. "I'm so sorry."

"We're in big trouble, James. My mom said a police officer is coming to school tomorrow to talk to us about it. And that we could get expelled or suspended." Matt's face turned white as all of the blood drained out of it. "I'm such an idiot!" cried Ruby. "I'm so stupid for thinking I could trust you! You know, people will forget about you in all of this after a few months. But it's me, it's my pictures that are gonna be online for *years* into the future."

"Ruby, I'm sorry. I didn't mean for this to happen, I-"
"Was it you that sent them out to everyone or someone else?"
James stared down at his shoes. "It was Matt," he said quietly.
"And how did Matt get them??" Ruby continued to cry.
"I sent them to him."
Several seconds of silence went between the two. "Just. Leave, James." Ruby quickly went inside and slammed the door, leaving James alone on the porch. "You shouldn't have sent them to me in the first place!" James yelled after her. She had a role in this too. James walked angrily home.

...

The police came to Oak Street Middle the next morning. Students watched and whispered as Ruby and James' names were called over the intercom. A few minutes later, Matt and several of the soccer boys were also called into the office.

Principal Spitz sat in his grey roller chair, looking very unhappy.

"This is...unfortunate." He told the students. "Ruby and James, I'll talk to you first. The rest of you can wait outside my office." He motioned for Ruby and James to step forward, and led the pair into a room filled with their parents' glaring, concerned stares. "Take a seat," said Spitz.

After

It took Ruby years to move past the pictures that were leaked during her eighth-grade year. Ruby gained a reputation that she liked being with lots of boys and was called a lot of awful names. Boys viewed her as a body, instead of a person, and many girls at school were mean to Ruby too. The soccer boys were especially awful because they had community service hours and Ruby didn't get an official punishment. Principal Spitz thought that the spreading of Ruby's pictures was punishment enough.

Ruby would cry herself to sleep every night and grew tired of feeling like there was no way out of the situation. Eventually, her parents decided it would be good if Ruby switched schools. Things got a little better after that. Even with the change of schools, the pictures popped up randomly all the way through high school. Only when Ruby moved out of state to go to college, she felt she could truly be free from the content she'd created. But in the back of her mind, she always wondered where her pictures remained in the dark, dusty corners of the internet, or saved on an old phone someone had tossed in the back of their closet.

Ruby also had a very hard time trusting people after James. Every time she went on a date with a boy, she worried that he was going to hurt her. It took years of going to therapy that finally helped Ruby feel like herself again, confident and strong.

James, after doing the 40 hours of community service Spitz sentenced him to, didn't think much of the incident with Ruby, except when he heard people gossiping about her or saw her in the hallways at school the rest of eighth grade. He never saw her again after middle school. But Ruby's eyes, broken and tear-stricken by his betrayal, were burned into James' memory. James remembered those eyes for the rest of his life.

Fifteen years after eighth grade, Ruby, who was just getting home from an extra-long orchestra rehearsal in the city, saw a letter in her mailbox.

Ruby,

I know I'm probably the very last person you want to hear from. I just wanted to tell you that I'm sorry. I'm so sorry, Ruby.

I have my own little girls now. They're two and four, and have bright red hair. I bring them out in my canoe sometimes, like we used to do all those years ago, with the autumn leaves falling around us like confetti. If someone hurts them like I hurt you, I would never forgive myself.

James

LET'S TALK!

Feel free to answer these questions either alone in your own thoughts, or with a group.

- This story was pretty heavy. How do you feel after reading it?
- Did you know that there were such big consequences for sending inappropriate pictures and videos?
- Have you ever known someone who experienced what Ruby went through? Without using anyone's names in the story, share it with those around you. What were their consequences?
- After reading James and Ruby's story, what is your opinion about sending inappropriate content? Would you ever consider sending it?
- Do you think the punishment James received was fair? Do you think Ruby should have been punished by the school?
- What could Ruby have done differently when James asked her for pictures?
- How did James manipulate Ruby into sending him the pictures?
- Can the inappropriate content Ruby created ever truly be deleted? Why or why not?
- What did you think about the ending of the story? What were the differences between Ruby's "after" and Jame's "after"?

92

HEALTHY WAYS TO USE TECH

Learn New Things

The internet is a fantastic place to learn new skills and research new ideas. You can learn millions, maybe even BILLIONS of things online! From learning a new language (Swahili anyone?), a new instrument, how to cook scrambled eggs, where to rent a hot air balloon, to knowing how many fish are in the sea (scientists think about 3,500,000,000,000 btw), the internet is an awesome place to figure out how to do real-world things.

Take Breaks and Tune In

Healthy tech users take a lot of breaks and know when to turn off the tech and tune in to the real world around them. Real-world events like birthdays, family dinners, and activities with friends are ALWAYS more important than screens. If you're having a really

from your screen, turn the power off and put it in another room.

Notifications can wait, but you'll never get back the memories you miss.

Delete the Apps

Delete any apps that are taking too much of your time, make you feel bad about yourself, or that you think you're addicted to. Don't worry if friends can't contact you anymore through these apps. If it's important enough, they'll find a way to reach out to you.

If you really don't want to delete an app, make a plan to only check it once per week for 15 minutes. Then you'll know that you can still be on the app, but that it can't take a huge chunk of your time.

Involve Your Family

Be open and honest about screen time with your family. Decide as a group when and where screens can be used, and for how long. Check the family discussion questions on page 88 to get the conversation started!

Be Open to Discussion and Use Tech as a Tool

Technology is going to continue to advance, and when you're old and gray, who knows what the new technology will be! That's why we must keep having important discussions about technology's role in our lives. You and your family must decide what values are important to you, and fit technology within those values. Don't let the internet and social media determine what's important in your life. Technology is a helpful tool that's available, it's not a road to happiness. Be in charge and in control of the technology you bring into your life; don't let technology control you.

Plan Real-World Activities

The internet is a great place to research fun places to go in real life! Plan a little trip with friends or family, something small in your town or city, that gets you all out of the house and out from behind the screens! You can look up restaurants, parks, stores, or anything else that sounds exciting and fun!

MINI QUIZ: ARE YOU READY FOR THE ONLINE WORLD?

1. How Old Are You?
a. Under 10 years old
b. 10-12
c. 13-15
d. 15+

2. What is the main reason you'd like to have a phone or other device?
a. I've never thought about that before!
b. Video games and meeting new people online
c. To talk with my friends anytime, anywhere. They're online all the time and I want to hang out with them
d. To connect online with friends and family, and to research school assignments or things I'm interested in

3. What would you do if you saw a classmate being cyberbullied?
a. Ignore it, it's none of your business!
b. Confront the bully on social media, and try to defend the person
c. Talk to the classmate and see if they need help
d. Talk to a parent or another trusted adult

4. How would you escape the online algorithm trap?
a. Cry
b. Just accept it. I don't see the big deal about the algorithms
c. I'll kind of try to make my settings private, but it's not that big of a deal
d. Change the privacy settings on my device, set my apps and websites to stop tracking my online activities, and be aware that websites are constantly trying to get my personal information

5. Who would you give your phone number to?
a. Anyone who asks! The more the merrier
b. Only people that I've been talking to online for a while
c. Anyone that I've met in person, even if I don't know them very well
d. My family, and only kind friends that I've met in person

6. Would you ever talk to someone you didn't know in person in an online game?
a. Yes, that's part of playing the game
b. Maybe? If they seemed nice and we were good at playing
c. Probably not, unless my real-world friend introduced us
d. No, I'd make a private server to play with only real-world friends

7. Would you ever meet up with someone you met online?
a. Sure! What's the worst that could happen?
b. Maybe? If they seemed really nice online and we'd been talking for a long time
c. Probably not, seem sketchy
d. Never. You never know the person behind the screen

8. How would you handle seeing a classmate post an inappropriate picture?
a. Screenshot it and send it to all of your friends
b. Look at it, but don't send it to anyone
c. Worry about it, then talk to your friends about what to do
d. Tell a parent or a trusted adult and ask their advice on what to do next

9. How do you balance school life and online activities?
a. There's no balance, I spend tons of time online after school and my grades are seriously not doing well :/
b. I really try, but sometimes I go into an internet black hole and five hours go by!
c. Ok? I get most of the stuff done that I need, but I find myself thinking about being online all of the time
d. Very good. I set specific times when I can be online and this allows me to get everything done that I need to

10. Do you have open family discussions about using the internet and the consequences that
a. Um no, never.
b. I'd like to, and maybe my family will in the future!
c. Sometimes? When we're in the mood.
d. Yes! All the time!

Mostly A's: You need to learn more about the online world before having a private device. Talk to your family about the steps you need to take and keep reading this book together!

Mostly B's: You are almost ready, but still need to learn a few more things. A great place to start is with the Family Discussion Questions on page 88.

Mostly C's: You're ready, but be careful. There are some things online you might not be 100% certain about. Always talk to a trusted adult if there's something online that doesn't make sense.

Mostly D's: You're very ready for the virtual world right! now! as long as you continue to be online-smart :)

My answers were mixed!: Seems like you're kinda ready and kinda not! There are some things that you need to learn before diving into the online world.

57 NON-TECH THINGS TO DO WHEN YOU'RE BORED

The World is BIG and WIDE. GO EXPLORE IT! It's really easy to sit your whole life behind a screen watching others explore the world around them. But what if I told you that YOU can explore the world someday right now?! Here are 57 screen-free ideas to help you kick-start your real-world adventures.

1. Read a good book

2. Write your name in cursive

3. Ask a friend to hang out

4. Ride a bike

5. Go to the local library

6. Bake cookies = YUM!

7. Play a board game

8. Go on a long walk with a family member

9. Plant a seed and watch it grow

10. Write a letter to a grandparent or distant relative

11. Have a sleepover!

12. Create a scavenger hunt

13. Play with a pet or your neighbor's pet

14. Organize your room or workspace

15. Write a short story about a magic rock that transports you anywhere you'd like to go

16. Go swimming at the pool

17. Make ice cream in a bag!

18. Tie-dye an old white shirt

19. Practice your sports skills

20. Ask a neighbor if they have a job you can do

21. Pick up the leaves and weeds in an elderly neighbor's yard (ask them first!)

22. Teach your dog a new trick (or your cat)

23. Bury some treasure and give someone the map

24. Create a blanket fort

25. Practice calligraphy

26. Watch the stars and think about how small you are in comparison with the rest of the universe

27. Make a dream journal

28. Water balloon fight!

29. Play flashlight tag

30. Play Pictionary

31. Go fishing

32. Make a scrapbook with some family photos (ask your parents first)

33. Bake a delicious cake

34. Paint a picture of a futuristic world

35. Write a kind note to your favorite teacher

36. Practice your instrument (or learn a new instrument!)

37. Make an obstacle course and see how fast you can run through it

38. Play in some sprinklers

39. Have a spa day with a nice bath/shower and a face mask

40. Learn how to tie different kinds of knots

41. Write down your bucket list of things you want to do before you graduate from high school

42. Do a puzzle

43. Go rock hunting

44. Call your grandparents, or another relative and ask them how they're doing (no texting!)

45. Get out a dictionary and discover your favorite word

46. Make a sign for your bedroom door or another personal space

47. Ask your parents for a job to do around the house to earn some extra money

48. Pick some wildflowers (if it's summer)

49. Build a snowman (if it's winter)

50. Paint some rocks and leave them around town

51. Go ice/roller skating

52. Make some smores

53. Redecorate or rearrange your room or personal space

54. Go grocery shopping with a parent

55. Try the ancient art of origami

56. Practice some yoga

57. Have a cupcake-decorating competition with some friends

Family Discussion Questions

1. What was technology like when our oldest family members were growing up? How has technology changed over time?

2. What are the capabilities of all of the devices we own? How can we use them and what are all of the tasks they can perform (e.g. taking pictures, used for texting, etc.)?

3. What are the reasons that each of us needs to use our devices?

4. What is our ideal day for our family and screen technologies?

5. Will parents monitor kid's devices with monitoring software?

6. Let's talk about screen time! How many minutes/hours do you think we should all be spending on our phones or devices? Is screen time earned through other tasks, or is it a basic right of everyone in the household?

7. In what areas of our house are we allowed to use tech?

8. At what age are video games allowed?

9. Will we play video games that contain violent things (guns, fighting, bad language, drugs, alcohol, etc.)?

10. What are some basic rules we should all follow when using our devices?

11. What should we do if we see something inappropriate online?

12. What should you do if someone else sends you an inappropriate text, picture, or video?

13. Is banning or blocking people online an okay thing to do? When is it okay and when is it not okay?

14. If an adult that you know tries contacting you online, should we talk about it to others? Why or why not?

15. What skills are we all great at? How could we use these skills online?

16. How do we think big tech and social media companies make money?

17. What is artificial intelligence?

18. What are the consequences of sending inappropriate content to others (whether the content is photos, videos, or inappropriate texts)?

19. What is hacking? Have any of our family members ever been hacked?

20. Should we, as a family, online shop? What should we shop online for?

21. Is it okay to click on an online ad?

22. What's our policy on passwords? Do we let each other know our passwords for things?

23. At what age should we have email addresses?

24. Will all of our family members have social media accounts? What age should we be allowed to use social media? What are some advantages and disadvantages of digital connections?

25. What should we do if a friend or classmate says they're going to hurt themselves or someone else on social media?

26. When are we going to have screen-free times? What time of day and on what occasions is it not okay to be on a screen?

27. What rules does school have for phones?

28. Will parents be monitoring the kids' online activities?

29. What should we do when we feel bad about looking at social media?

30. What kinds of things is it okay for us to post on social media? What is not okay?

31. Do the things we post online ever go away? Why could this be good or bad?

32. What is our secret family "code word" if someone contacts us on the phone or online and we don't know if it's real or not?

33. What should we do if someone uses A.I. to hurt or threaten us in some way?

34. Do we all feel comfortable relying on each other if we have questions, problems, or worries about future tech use?

35. What are some fun family activities we can do besides screen time?!

SOURCES

Bates, Philip. "5 Ways Hackers Use Public Wi-Fi to Steal Your Identity." MakeUseOf, 4 July 2022.

Bogna, John. "What Is the Environmental Impact of Cryptocurrency?" PCMag, 8 Jan. 2022.

"A Brief History of the Internet." Board of Regents of the University System of Georgia.

Flavin, Brianna. "Is Cyberbullying Illegal? When Comments Turn Criminal." Rasmussen University, 25 Apr. 2017.

Grizzard, Matthew, et al. "Being Bad in a Video Game Can Make Us More Morally Sensitive." Cyberpsychology, Behavior, and Social Networking, vol. 17, no. 8, 2014, pp. 499-504.

Hempe, Melanie. "A Call to Parents: The Screen Effect." Screen Strong, 23 July 2020.

Hempe, Melanie. "Are Video Games Making Our Kids Violent?" Screen Strong, 9 Aug. 2019.

Kardaras, Dr. Nicholas. "It's 'Digital Heroin': How Screens Turn Kids into Psychotic Junkies." New York Post, 29 Aug. 2016.

Kosoff, Maya. "Study: 420 Million People around the World Are Addicted to the Internet." Business Insider, 20 Dec. 2014.

Shao, Rong, and Yunqiang Wang. "The Relation of Violent Video Games to Adolescent Aggression: An Examination of Moderated Mediation Effect." Frontiers in Psychology, vol. 10, 2019.

Tate, Allison Slater. "Facebook Whistleblower Frances Haugen Says Parents Make 1 Big Mistake with Social Media." TODAY.com, 8 Feb. 2022.

Turner, Ash. "How Many People Have Smartphones Worldwide (July 2022)." BankMyCell, 30 June 2022.

Valdez, Rubi. "Heavy Screen Time May Cause Premature Changes in Brain Structure among Kids: Study." Tech Times, 10 Dec. 2018.

"Virtual Reality Definition & Meaning." Merriam-Webster.

THE
END

If you enjoyed this book, please kindly consider writing me an Amazon review. It really helps me to keep writing my stories!

- ♥ -

Made in the USA
Coppell, TX
18 February 2025

46103225R00057